Dorothy Cretcher

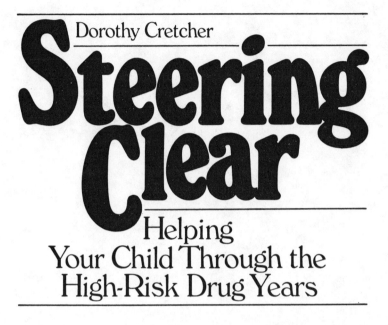

Steering Clear

Helping Your Child Through the High-Risk Drug Years

Foreword by Sidney Cohen, M.D.

Winston Press

Designed and produced by Art Direction, Inc.

Library of Congress Catalog Number: 82-60362

ISBN: 0-86683-689-6

Printed in the United States of America

5   4   3   2   1

Winston Press, Inc. 430 Oak Grove Minneapolis, MN 55403

ACKNOWLEDGEMENTS

If ever a manuscript was "developed," it was this one. It grew, stage by stage and version by version, as my knowledge and experience widened. Along the way, I became indebted to the many scholars, drug prevention and treatment specialists, parents, students, and others that I talked with or whose works I read. Many whose names do not appear here made contributions. Please know that I am deeply grateful to everyone who helped.

Many of the statistics that appear in the book are from the annual survey of high school seniors conducted under the direction of Dr. Lloyd Johnston by the Institute for Social Research at the University of Michigan. Dr. H. Stephen Glenn, Director of the Pacific Institute for Family Development, Bethesda, Maryland, not only contributed ideas but influenced the tone and posture of the manuscript. I am especially grateful to the many drug prevention and treatment specialists who sent personal letters, pamphlets, books, bibliographies, and other information along with their responses to my questionnaire. Thanks are also due the school principals who permitted me to interview their students and to the students, who were frank and helpful.

A number of manuscript reviewers made invaluable contributions to the development process. The entire manuscript was reviewed by Sue A. Polzella, former Assistant to the Director, Youth Drug Program of Montgomery County, Ohio; by Tom Arnold, Director, and Karen Neff, Education Specialist, Bureau of Alcoholism Services (BAS), Montgomery County, Ohio; by Thomas Croke, Lifeline Project,

Saint Anne's Hospital, Fall River, Massachusetts; by Amos Clifford, Program Director, Mainstreet Youth Program, Turning Point, Visalia, California; by Paul Fishbein, The Phoenix House Foundation, New York City; and by staff members of the National Institute on Drug Abuse. In addition, individual chapters were reviewed as follows:

Chapter four ("Alcohol and Tobacco") was reviewed by Dr. H. Stephen Glenn; and by Kerry Newman, Alcoholism Treatment Counselor, BAS.

Chapter six ("The Other Drugs") was reviewed by Dr. Leonard T. Sigell, Director, The Drug and Poison Information Center, University of Cincinnati Medical Center; and by Susan Guntren, R.Ph., Coordinator, Western Ohio Regional Poison and Drug Information Center.

Most of the material that eventually became chapters seven and eight ("Prevention: What You Can Do" and "Dealing With the Drug Use of Your Child") was reviewed by John Toto, Director, the Bridge Therapeutic Center, Philadelphia; by James Lakehomer, Psychologist, Lane County Mental Health Division, Drug Treatment Program, Eugene, Oregon; by Kerry Newman; and by Stephen Glenn, who also contributed original source material and references.

Special thanks are due Mark Johnson, who provided not only legwork but enthusiasm. As always, I am indebted to my husband, Dick, who offered ideas, interest, and support. Above all, I am grateful to Bill Pflaum, whose involvement, guidance, optimism and tenacity fueled the project throughout.

FOREWORD

Sidney Cohen, M.D.

Clinical Professor of Psychiatry
Neuropsychiatric Institute
U.C.L.A. School of Medicine

It was with mixed feelings that I began to read *Steering Clear*. How can a subject as complicated as adolescent drug abuse be understandably and accurately dealt with by a layperson? How could the many dilemmas confronting today's parents be sensibly resolved?

It seems that Dorothy Cretcher has brought it off. The information is correct and up-to-date. The parental guidance is balanced and reasonable. The underlying theme is that a skillful attempt to reweave the torn fabric of parent-child misunderstandings, and to redirect dysfunctional behaviors into healthier patterns must take place.

What can be added to the text? Very little, except to underline some of the points of special salience to me.

The setting of limits and providing of responsibilities (lovingly) must start very early. To confront a teenager who has been brought up without particular guidance or in an overly permissive manner with a set of fixed house rules, can be explosive. Children actually want guidelines. If parents do not provide them, they will seek them out from others, sometimes to their detriment.

One wonders: At what age should young people make decisions about drug usage that can affect them for a lifetime? At present some pre-teenagers are either making such decisions or slipping unthinkingly into a life style that can lead to future mental blunting or physical impairment. It seems clear that children must be dissuaded from destructive drug use at least until they are capable of making their own informed judgments. Therefore parental intervention is necessary until a certain measure of maturity has been achieved.

From the book it turns out that the problem is not only drugs although they are usually a most visible signal. The problems are a rapidly changing society that has lost its viable goals and values, parents who have either neglected or overprotected their offspring, children who have (naturally) mimicked the behaviors of the most deviant of their peers or role models.

Some of this use of chemicals to alter awareness, distort perception, unrestrain conduct, evade stress and seek instant pleasure is new and different. But to keep it all in perspective we must remember that Socrates (470-399 BC) expressed concern about "the young men of Athens with their long hair, their indolence and their disdain for adult values." And long before that an Egyptian papyrus when translated read, "Our earth is degenerate — children no longer obey their parents."

CONTENTS

Chapter One

Young people and drugs
An Overview

The drug problem sneaked up on us. It may seem strange to our children, but most of our generation grew up without laying eyes on a joint or a Quaalude. Adolescent drug use was almost unknown in our day. Now we're told that our kids live in a world of pushers and junkies who shoot up, freak out. O.D., and no doubt do other things just as outrageous. We hear that drugs pose a serious threat to the health and well-being, and sometimes even the lives of our children. *Of course* we're confused, scared, and threatened.

The natural reaction is to try not even to think about kids having drug problems. It's like the possibility of getting cancer or causing an accident that seriously injures someone. If, God forbid, our own kids got involved in drugs, we'd have to work through a tough family problem for which we are woefully unprepared. As if that weren't enough trouble, we might find ourselves doubting the value of the huge part of ourselves we've poured into raising our children. Maybe we made some dreadful mistake that canceled out all the time, effort, and love we invested.

Another perfectly normal response to drug problems is simply not to believe our own kids are affected. A lot of us take this approach. A recent survey conducted by a midwestern school system found that 78 percent of the district's parents believed marijuana was a serious problem in the schools. But only 17 percent believed their own kids were involved! The truth was that more than half of the students in grades seven to twelve had tried marijuana, and almost a third were regular users.

There is still another attitude we bring to the drug problem that makes it hard to handle. A little quiz will demonstrate this pitfall. Can you identify the drug that a) is most used and abused by adolescents, b) often leads to serious physical and mental disorders, c) can be fatal in a single overdose, and d) is addictive and causes severe withdrawal symptoms when its use is discontinued? The answer is not heroin or PCP or LSD, but old familiar alcohol. At the same time that we're panic-stricken by drugs unfamiliar to us, most of us take in stride one that is just as great a menace. It's as if we're scared to death of alligators, but make pets of crocodiles.

I myself have experienced all the reactions to drug use I've been describing. When my own kids were in high school, it never occurred to me they might use drugs. They were far too well brought up and exceptional. Later on, when our son came home from college and told us he'd tried cocaine, I was stunned into silence. My son, realizing that silence was not a normal condition in me, quickly apologized — for telling me! And we dropped the subject. That same evening, we all had a drink together, without any stunned silence or heart palpitations on my part. *Several years later*, we had our first real family talk about drugs.

To atone for my sins of omission, I have recently learned a great deal about drug use among adolescents. It hasn't always been easy. For one thing, the experts sometimes don't agree with each other. For another, neither young people nor social scientists seem to be speaking English. The kids talk about overamping, luding out, and doing damage to roaches. The scientists speak of enabling (which is bad), habilitating (which is good), and somatosensory affectional deprivation (which is unintelligible, as far as I know).

But now I think I have deciphered the Rosetta stone of drug conversation, whether of those who do drugs or of those who analyze and diagnose the doers. I have plodded through reams of ponderous research papers and have indexed them on little cards the way our English teachers said to. I have talked with young people and with drug care professionals. I have surveyed more than 130 drug treatment and prevention agencies. And I can report to you, in brief now and in detail later, that:

● Drug use among adolescents is a widespread, serious peril. Along with other problems that also have erupted during the past decade, it is a real threat to the health, welfare, and development of our children.

● The problem is not too frightful to be considered. In some ways, we're luckier than the parents who tried to cope with drug use just before us. We know the score now. National surveys of drug use among high school seniors have been conducted annually for several years by a team at the University of Michigan, and there have been many other studies. We also have some reliable information about the physical and mental dangers that drugs pose to adolescents. And, most encouraging, we now have some resources for dealing with the situation. Programs have begun to appear that have been successful both in treating and preventing drug problems among children and adolescents.

● No parent whose kids get into trouble with drugs should waste time feeling guilty. Young people who've had the finest upbringing have been known to yield to the enormous pressures to use drugs that they face outside the family. At the same time, there are some things parents can do to protect their children. The first step is to understand the adolescent drug situation—an undertaking to which I can lend a hand.

Some Preliminary Business

In the interest of orderliness, let's begin by defining what a drug is. Webster offers several definitions, but the one that applies here is "a substance other than food intended to affect the structure or function of the body." Aspirin, antacids, caffeine, nicotine, and alcohol are drugs that are legal and accepted in our society. (At least two of them have done a lot of damage.) Other legal substances used and abused by young people include glue, gasoline, sleep medications, cough medicine, and various products like paint and hairspray sold in aerosol cans. Other drugs that kids are using can be divided into illegal drugs (marijuana, LSD, cocaine) and prescription drugs used without a prescription (amphetamines, barbiturates, tranquilizers). Some of the latter are produced illegally in bootleg laboratories. I will sometimes lump together under the heading "illicit drugs" all substances that have a potential for abuse and are used in ways not sanctioned by society. The term "illicit drugs" does not include alcohol and tobacco.

Drugs also can be classified by their functions. LSD, PCP, and mescaline are hallucinogens or psychedelics — that is, they make changes in the way the user experiences color, sound, time, space, and other realities. Marijuana is classified as a mild hallucinogen. Other categories include stimulants (caffeine, cocaine, amphetamines) and depressants (alcohol, tranquilizers, barbiturates and other sedatives). Narcotics (heroin, codeine, Demerol, methadone) are strong drugs that have a calming effect, tend to induce sleep, and are dangerously addictive.

Another issue that needs to be dealt with at the outset is the difference between drug use and abuse. Some people use those terms interchangeably. They believe "all use is abuse," particularly when the user is an adolescent. What I think the slogan means is "all drug use should be taken seriously." If so, I agree wholeheartedly. But that doesn't mean it's necessary, or likely to be helpful, to panic the first time you find a joint in a youngster's bedroom. (What you should do at that point, in my opinion, is have a very serious but friendly conversation with the child, taking care both to listen to his or her point of view and to convey your own position clearly. Make sure your kids know how you feel about drug use, why you feel that way, and what behavior you expect in the future.)

My own view is that it's best to distinguish between use and abuse because doing so will improve parents' credibility with children and because experimentation needs to be dealt with differently than more frequent use (see chapter eight). Therefore, for the purposes of this book, *drug abuse* means the use of any drug to the point that it damages the user's health, job, education, personal relationships, judgment, or ability to cope with daily life. *Drug use* is anything short of that, but should not be understood to imply approval.

The Bad News

During the 1970s, adolescent drug use spread around the country like a nasty virus. At the beginning of the decade, only 20 percent of high school senior boys (girls weren't counted in those days) had used an illicit drug at some time in their lives. By 1981, that figure had more than tripled to 66 percent of all seniors, boys and girls included. When use of alcohol is added, the graph goes through the ceiling. Ninety-three percent of the class of 1981 had at least tried alcohol.

Those figures are alarming because of their size and because they represent a trend, to put it mildly. But they include kids who have used drugs only once or twice in their lifetimes. To learn the extent of more serious drug use, you'll need to sit still for some more statistics from the annual national survey of high school seniors:

• More than 20 percent of recent high school seniors had used illicit drugs on a regular basis.

• Seven percent of the 1981 graduating class (one of every fourteen seniors) used marijuana daily. About a third of this group smoked four or more joints per day, all but assuring they were high during school hours.

• Forty-one percent of the class of '81 had been drunk during the two weeks just before the survey.

Nor are drugs by any means confined to high school upperclassmen. More than half of the teenagers who use marijuana had their first experience in the ninth grade or earlier. The first big initiation takes place in the seventh grade. Alcohol is used not only by more kids overall, but by more at earlier ages. Alcohol is the gateway drug—the one that kids use first. By the time they finish the ninth grade, 56 percent of all teenagers have tried it. Cigarettes, glue, and aerosol products are also popular among younger children.

Every adult responsible for children needs to know that chances for exposure to drug use range from excellent to almost certain. More than 80 percent of all high school seniors, for example, report that some of their friends smoke marijuana. It would hardly be easier to get drugs if they were sold in the pop machine. Almost every youngster knows how and where to get them.

What about the decrease in drug use you've been reading about in the newspapers? A recent headline in my hometown paper read "Drug Culture Burning Itself Out." Unfortunately, the story that followed wasn't quite so optimistic. It's true that a decrease in the use of marijuana began in 1980. Any decline is good news and this one is doubly encouraging because it seems to be tied, at least in part, to the number of young people who believe marijuana involves a health risk. It indicates that kids respond to information. A much sharper drop in regular cigarette smoking also seems to be related to health information.

Beyond those modest signs, however, there isn't much to inspire hopeful headlines. For one thing, the decrease is partial. The decline in daily marijuana smoking in the early eighties was considered significant and it was welcome, but it represented only a few steps down the long staircase climbed by daily smokers during the 1970s. Another piece of bad news is that the average marijuana cigarette today is four times as potent as the ones the kids smoked in the early seventies. It's also true that use of illicit drugs other than marijuana (particularly stimulants) continued to rise rather sharply in 1980-81. We still have what the authors of the high school survey call "probably the highest levels of illicit drug use among young people of any industrialized nation in the world."

Drug use statistics translate into tragedy in the lives of children. Even marijuana, the one drug we thought might be harmless, has turned out to involve serious health risks. At the end of the seventies, the United States Surgeon General reported a fall in the death rate of all groups of Americans, except adolescents and young adults. During the same years that young people were turning to drugs in record numbers, their death rate rose and (by their own assessment) their health deteriorated. The leading cause of death for the age-group was alcohol-related car accidents. One of their major health problems was alcoholism. They went to the doctor most often for respiratory ailments, which can be linked to marijuana and tobacco smoking.

Unfortunately, poor health is not the only ill effect of drug use among adolescents. Any drug counselor can tell stories about whole families whose lives are disrupted by the drug abuse of a youthful member or by an unfortunate family response to a drug problem. Struggles over drugs can damage family relationships.

Young people who are less seriously involved with drugs may nonetheless miss out on important experiences of transition from child to adult that normally take place during adolescence. Kids who cope with life through drugs may never learn to cope on a healthier basis. Youngsters who are regularly spaced out may one day find themselves adults without skills to solve personal problems, make decisions, or function in social and professional situations. They also may lack more mundane abilities like math and typing. Research laboratories are now reporting what teachers have long known — that kids who are drug and alcohol abusers are seriously hampered in the classroom.

There is some alarming evidence that drug abuse is only one part of a bigger problem among adolescents. As a group, our children are floundering in larger waters. The second leading cause of death for nonwhite youths during the seventies was murder; for whites, it was suicide. The rate of violent crime among those under eighteen increased by more than 40 percent during the decade. In addition to alcohol and drug abuse, the leading health problems of the age-group are violent death and injury, sexually transmitted diseases, and unwanted pregnancy. About one of every ten teenage girls becomes pregnant each year, and two-thirds of these expectant mothers are unmarried. As if that weren't enough trouble, various studies tell us that a large number of young people in their twenties lack adequate skills to make a living or run a home and family.

The message in that catalog of horrors is that we need to treat the disease as well as the symptoms. We must address the deeper troubles behind drug abuse. I've reached the conclusion that adults should concentrate most on helping kids develop the stability and skills to cope with life in an unsettled era. The solution to drug and other adolescent problems, in my opinion, lies first and foremost in the family, then in the schools and other points of contact between young people and adults. I think everything we do with our children should aim at helping them prepare to function independently in a world of change and pressure.

Now for the good news: we can do it. Kids can be helped to successfully navigate the adolescent years, even during the eighties. Thirty-four percent of all teenagers have no involvement with illicit drugs whatsoever. The decline in cigarette and marijuana smoking, due in part to health information, is further encouragement.

Parenting is a tough but forgiving business. It's possible to make a thousand blunders and still turn out young people who can function not only adequately but well in our society. The trick is to understand the process, aim in the right direction, and keep trying. Many ordinary families are doing it. Some of their secrets are shared in this book's final chapters, along with other suggestions for dealing with drug-related problems in the family, the schools, and the community.

Chapter Two

How did this happen to us?

The current drug epidemic among teenagers began somewhere around 1965. Before that time, illicit drugs in our country were pretty much confined to minorities, people with unconventional lifestyles, and soldiers stationed in drug-using countries. The children of middle-class America rarely heard about drugs, and they certainly didn't use them.

Then how did we get to a state of crisis in little more than a decade? There have been many explanations and proposed solutions, ranging from stamping out rock music to seminars on getting high on life. The analysis that follows is one I've put together from many sources, including my own observation. It describes some of the changes in our society that prepared the ground for drug use and abuse to grow in. The changes are not necessarily in order of importance. While solutions to drug problems are dealt with in a more orderly arrangement elsewhere, a few starter suggestions follow each section here. None of these is a foolproof remedy for drug use. They're simply common-sense ways to try to moderate the climate that drug problems have grown so well in.

Our Drug Mentality. You only need watch TV for an evening to realize that our society has a pill for every problem. Beginning with baby aspirin, we teach our children to look for a chemical cure for any disorder. We expect

9

everything from colds to cancer to be cured by drugs, if not now, then as soon as science makes the breakthrough.

Nor is our faith in drugs limited to physical disorders. Television characters who are upset these days not only take a drink, but have a Valium. There are pills to pep us up, calm us down, put us to sleep, wake us up, and keep us from worrying. Cocaine is just one logical (if giant) step beyond the colas that promise to keep us "feelin' good." Feeling good, by the way, is the number one reason given by youngsters for the use of almost every illicit drug.

What can you do? Watch what unspoken messages about drugs the adults in your family are sending the children. Take a hard look at your own use of tobacco, alcohol, or tranquilizers. Don't push legal drugs on children unless you absolutely have to. Teach young children that medicine is to be used only in case of illness, and then very cautiously. Be sure they clearly understand the differences among aspirin, flavored vitamins, and candy. When it's possible, try nonchemical solutions (relaxation therapy for headaches, for example) for physical problems.

Changes in the Family. Families haven't grown weaker because we are bad parents. But we do struggle against odds, brought on by larger social changes, that our grandparents didn't dream of. We are one of the first generations in history to try raising children without the help of grandparents, aunts and uncles, close friends and neighbors. The result is a huge strain on one or two sets of what may be quite ordinary shoulders.

In very recent times, the challenge of parenting has become even more concentrated. It often falls on a single person, who also has the full responsibility for earning a living, running a home, and maintaining a personal life. Where there are two parents, chances are good that both are out of the home during working hours, often for the sake of making economic ends meet. In both cases, the time that parents can spend with children is limited and likely to be overhung with fatigue and harassment. Some families, of course, manage beautifully, but the point is that it isn't easy.

In addition to its loss of size, time, and shared responsibility, the family has lost some functions that used to give it clout with children. Parents no longer teach kids how to make a living, as they did when we were a country of farmers, mom and pop stores, and cottage industries. Few people take up their parents' occupations. Young people may go through years of complex training for careers that didn't exist when we were learning to be teachers, mechanics, and accountants.

Rapid change has also outdated us in other areas. Parents are no longer the experts who introduce children to the ways of the world. We're in the dark about a lot of things, from the inner workings of the video game to international economics. We sometimes can't even teach our kids the simple but true modern essentials like where to find the nearest shopping center, because we change towns so often. Parents no longer have automatic status as authorities.

We can contribute to our loss of authority by being overly permissive or by overzealously trying to be our children's friends. We may hesitate to give our kids strong guidance for fear of squelching their independent spirits or losing their friendship. If so, our kids will be quick to pick up on the message we're sending: don't think of us as authorities.

The loss of parental influence is critical because of its relationship to serious drug problems. Kids who come from strong, cohesive families are much less likely to get into trouble with drugs. Therefore, chapter seven of this book has a section on discouraging drug problems at the family level. Meanwhile, anything you can do to strengthen your family life will be helpful. Spend all the time you can with your children. Talk with them. Eat with them. Work with them. Learn with them. Influence them whenever you can. Remember that, at the very least, you have one all-essential thing to teach them: how to be a decent, grown-up human being.

Changes in Community. You probably remember, when you were a kid, how the news of your mischief got home before you did. Today, if your child gets into trouble more than three doors from home, the residents probably won't even know him. He or she is much more likely to encounter a hostile stranger than a father or mother figure. Among the people we do know, many of us parents are too eager to keep up appearances to discuss our problems. The neighbors seem to think they have perfect children, so we pretend ours are perfect, too.

Close-knit communities used to provide not only support for both parents and children, but a strong incentive to walk the straight and narrow. Status in the community was a family affair. Kids who got into more than the permissible amount of trouble lost status among their peers, who were reflecting their parents. It wasn't a perfect system, but it tended to enforce community standards. Today our children have both the blessings and the dangers of not knowing the neighbors. We can't count on the community to look after our kids.

Probably the best way you can build a community that will help with drug problems is to get to know the parents of your children's friends. In some places, parents have gotten together for the specific purpose of combating drug problems among their own children. These new communities have rediscovered that there's strength in numbers and that it's easier for kids to accept restrictions when their friends have also been reined in. One such successful experiment is described in a book, *Parents Peers and Pot*, by Marsha Manatt, described in the bibliography following chapter eight.

The Nature of Adolescence. The word *adolescence* only dates from about 1900. Before that time, most people went right from childhood into the labor force. After child labor was outlawed, kids in rural America still had real responsibilities. They were necessary to their families' economic survival. Even in towns, families spent a lot of time together in essential activities like gardening, canning, sewing, and firing the furnace. Recreation also took place at home or in the nearby community, with adults and kids in close contact.

Today, we don't need children for anything. Even the garbage goes down the disposal. Not only does this pull an important human rug (the need to be needed) out from under our kids, but it means there are few natural opportunities for young people and adults to come together around important activities.

As a result, young people turn to each other sooner than they used to. During the same years that family and community ties were weakening, adolescent society was growing stronger. Partly as a legacy of the sixties, children who reach adolescence find a full-blown youth culture, with its own clothing, music, language and (most important) values. During the years when human beings are most curious and least cautious, our kids are influenced mainly by each other. During the time when most humans make the transition from looking for status and acceptance from their parents to their peers, these young people are confronted by what may be history's most intense peer pressure. Unfortunately, much of that peer pressure is prodrug.

The gap between the adolescent and adult worlds can complicate the naturally tricky business of reaching adulthood. Kids want to be independent and in step with their peer society. Adults, who see that their children are still immature in many ways, resist giving up control. The result can be perpetual conflict that makes it difficult for parents to help, influence, or even hold a normal conversation with their children during the adolescent years. Or, at the other extreme, parents may throw up their hands and give kids more freedom than they're able to handle, often along with a dose of unhealthy hostility.

What's a parent to do? If your kids are still toddlers or

elementary-school children, prepare yourself with some training for parenthood. Courses now are available in most communities. If a youngster of yours has already reached adolescence, work hard at the transition to being the parent of an adult. Gradually, hand over the reins. Sort out areas in which you must remain the authority (no drugs, for example) from those your kids can manage (an ever larger number of self-responsibilities as they grow older). If you're having trouble with a family power struggle, arrange some counseling or other outside help.

Spend all the time you can with your children, preferably in activities with purpose. Going to the movies is okay; camping is better; painting the house together would be terrific. It's the principle that's important — you can work out the details to fit your family's interests and resources.

Organize your household so that kids have real responsibilities. We had an orchard and truck patch that took care of that problem for us. There was some grumbling, but no one felt unneeded at our house during apple season. You can accomplish the same thing with household duties. If your older children get home before you do in the afternoon, give them the responsibility for dinner, the laundry, or whatever needs doing at your house. The trick is to use duties that are clearly essential. One single working parent, Eleanor Berman, wrote a book about how her children blossomed as they took over household responsibilities. Ms. Berman's book, *The Cooperating Family*, is described in the bibliography.

Encourage your kids to bring home their friends, no matter how scroungy. (Remember that many an honest heart beats beneath an outrageous tee shirt.) If they're going to influence each other, let them do it at your house, where you may be able to put a word in on behalf of moderation.

Changes in the Schools. School is the headquarters of adolescent society. Kids spend the largest part of their time there. Most of their influential peer relationships are worked out in or near the school, often in a cloud of smoke that smells suspiciously like marijuana.

Schools are beset by problems. We expect far too much of them, and they deliver too little. Their size alone makes them hard to handle. Teachers who deal with thirty different students every hour can't begin to know them. We've had a tendency to use our schools as a dumping ground for all problems that affect young people, from sex to summer employment. In the early eighties, budget cuts are compounding the difficulties. Teachers and school officials feel harassed and put upon. Kids feel powerless, oppressed by rules that seem silly to them, and disrespectful. One more important adult influence has fallen.

One thing that schools don't teach very well (nor do many parents) is how to make decisions. Any child can tell you that, at school, decisions are made for you. Kids who haven't learned to decide for themselves are vulnerable to pressure, which is available by the truckload from the peer group.

Solving the problems of the schools is far beyond my scope or understanding. It probably won't help to move to a "better" school district, since many excellent school systems have trouble with drugs. The most important thing to be aware of is that your school doesn't have the time or resources to solve your community's drug problem, without a lot of help from you and other quarters.

Alienation and Affluence. Neither of these factors has much bearing on current adolescent drug use, but both were important when the problem was incubating during the sixties. The flower children were generally well funded. They had enough money to travel around the country, survive without jobs in places like Haight-Ashbury, buy drugs, and make bail when they got busted. They also were in open rebellion against their parents, middle-class society, and a government they thoroughly distrusted. The protesters of the sixties believed "the system" was waging a criminal war with one hand and throwing them in jail for using marijuana with the other. Flaunting drugs became as important as opposing war in the protest movement. The drugs spread across the country on college campuses and filtered down to high school, where the ground had been made fertile by the changes described in this chapter.

We can't undo the sixties, and not many of us are looking for a cure for affluence, but whatever part alienation may still be playing in drug use can be dealt with. Alienation sets in when people give up on changing anything. Any opportunity you can give your kids to bring about a change *that matters to them* is likely to be helpful. Listen to their legitimate complaints about the way your family functions and, when you can, let them help work out solutions. If your kids are like mine, for example, they probably insist the family chores aren't divided fairly. The next time that happens, invite them to join you in working out a new duty plan that is fair to everyone, including parents. Kids can be given a voice in many family problems and decisions. Not only will participation make them feel effective, but it will give them practice in decision making and responsibility. It also may result in more effective problem solving than we would anticipate.

From here it gets tougher, but parents can sometimes help young people find or organize groups to deal with bite-sized parts of important problems like conservation, neighborhood cleanup, or political action. Kids who've helped to change things are rarely afflicted with futility.

One remnant of the sixties among today's youth is mistrust of both the government and the news media, two major sources of drug information. This history of mistrust makes it essential to get your facts straight when you talk with kids about drugs. Don't tell them that marijuana will turn their brains into jello. The established facts don't need help to make a strong case against the use of drugs by adolescents.

Uncertainty About the Future. Young people aren't the only ones with doubts about the future. The bomb has been joined by some new worries. We're all aware our current way of life is at the mercy of the world supply of oil. We're threatened by inflation, crime, and faltering institutions. In addition, teenagers have some well-justified doubts about their personal futures. What are their chances in a job market geared to high technology? Will they be able to cope in a roller coaster society? Why sacrifice feeling good today to avoid lung cancer somewhere down a road that may be going nowhere?

I don't have the answers to those questions. We can't protect ourselves, let alone our children, from the uncertainties of the time we live in. But what we can do is provide one basic certainty: our relationships with them. Kids who know they can count on their parents, even when they're off the course their parents may have charted for them, have a special rudder. That is the one security we can guarantee them.

Rock Music. There is a relationship between drugs and rock music. The variety called acid rock actually grew out of the drug experience. The lyrics of some rock songs celebrate drug use. Rock stars have flaunted their use of drugs onstage before crowds of youthful fans. Rock concerts are notorious for their drug sidewalk sales, and the popular wisdom is that you can get high at a concert simply by breathing.

But none of those connections means that young people who like rock are sure to use drugs, any more than liking country music means they'll drink or have miserable love lives. Thousands of kids listen to rock music without using drugs.

Some parents' organizations have declared war on rock as part of their anti-drug programs. I have some serious misgivings about that approach. I think attacking young people's music is much more likely to polarize families than to reduce drug use. If anything, I think rock would sound better to kids if it were forbidden. A more helpful idea, in my opinion, is to talk with your children about the "drugs are dandy" messages in rock songs, along with those they hear on TV and in the movies.

Rock concerts are a different matter. I think I'd try to keep youngsters away from them. Or, if the group is too important to miss, volunteer to chaperone a carload of concert goers. Your kids won't be overjoyed with the arrangement, but they'll probably decide it's better than not going. If you've had the foresight to set up a parent community or network, use it to arrive at a group strategy. The medicine will go down easier if the whole gang has to take it. Some activist parent groups have also been able to convince concert hall officials to crack down on drugs at concerts.

Availability. It's obvious that people who can't get drugs don't use them. It's also true that people are more likely to try drugs when they're surrounded by them—the situation our kids face today. Drugs are abundantly available to children.

An obvious course is to step up law enforcement, and we should indeed support police efforts to reduce the supply of drugs to our children. But we can't look to the police, any more than to the schools, for a complete solution. Our law enforcement agencies are already overloaded. There isn't room in our jails for a quarter of the country's drug dealers. The borders that drugs are smuggled over are far too long and unprotected, the sources of drugs are far too numerous and varied, and the drug business is far too profitable to yield to the law without a long, expensive struggle. Our kids can't wait that long for a solution.

We need to accept the fact that drugs are not going to be stamped out soon enough to matter to the current crop of children. The challenge to parents is to prepare children to handle themselves even when they're surrounded by drug use. We must help them learn to navigate shark-filled waters, since there's no way we can harpoon all the sharks.

Chapter Three

The who, what and why of adolescent drug use

Back in the forties and fifties, the word drugs usually brought heroin to mind. During the sixties, it usually meant LSD and marijuana. Today, it conjures up a host of pills and powders from angel dust to Valium. As times change and the list grows longer, adults have more opportunity to be confused. Those who are bewildered about which drugs kids are choosing from the current smorgasbord can take heart, however—information is on the way. Here are some highlights from recent national surveys:

• The drug most used and abused by today's youth is the one it always has been: alcohol. Nearly all (93 percent) of the nation's high school seniors had tried alcohol at some time and more than 70 percent had used it during the month just before the 1981 survey. More than 40 percent reported having five or more drinks in a row during the preceding two weeks. And almost 30 percent said that all or most of their friends get drunk at least once a week. No other drug can match that record.

• Marijuana is the illicit drug that adolescents use by far most often. Even after the decline in marijuana use at the beginning of the eighties, 60 percent of the senior class had tried it; almost a third classified themselves as current users; and seven percent reported smoking daily.

• The use of other illicit drugs (stimulants, depressants, hallucinogens, and others) as a group increased at a slow but steady pace during the seventies. It is significant that this increase accelerated as marijuana use began to drop in the early eighties.

Although boys use more drugs overall, girls have been catching up in the "other illicit drugs" category. By 1981, girls were slightly more likely than boys to go beyond marijuana in their drug use. The seniors who have done so (more than 40 percent of the total class) are most likely to have used one of the stimulants known on the street as speed.

• Individual drugs rise and fall in popularity. After more than doubling from 1976-79, the growth in cocaine use began to slow down in the early eighties in the southern and north central states. The popularity of PCP, which swept the country during the seventies, dropped sharply in 1980-81 as its bad reputation grew.

At the same time, the use of stimulants (including amphetamines, counterfeit amphetamines, and over-the-counter products) increased sharply, particularly among girls. The sedative methaqualone (Quaaludes), which spread rapidly throughout the late seventies, continued its rise at a slower rate in the early eighties. In addition to their national ups and downs, drug fads come and go in particular communities and areas of the country.

• Information on the daily use of drugs is important because daily users are most likely to run into health and safety problems. Tobacco is the drug most used by seniors on a daily basis. Surprisingly, more girls than boys are heavy smokers. A slightly larger percentage of seniors use marijuana than alcohol on a daily basis, although more students use alcohol overall (that is, on measures of lifetime, annual, and monthly use). What seems to be going on here is that marijuana is the "everyday" drug, used something like tobacco, while alcohol is more often reserved for weekend binges.

With the exception of stimulants at 1.2 percent, each of the other illicit drugs is used daily by less than one percent of the national senior class. Before we chalk up a victory, however, we need to be aware that one percent of that single high school class represents 30,000 young people.

DRUG USE, CLASS OF 1981

(Figures indicate the percentage of high school seniors who have used each drug ever, annually, monthly, and on a daily basis.)

	Ever Used	Used in Past Year	Used in Past Month	Use Daily
Alcohol	92.6	87.0	70.7	6.0
Tobacco	71.0	NA	29.4	20.3
Marijuana	59.5	46.1	31.6	7.0
Stimulants	32.2	26.0	15.8	1.2
Cocaine	16.5	12.4	5.8	.3
Hallucinogens	15.7	10.1	4.4	.1
Sedatives	16.0	10.5	4.6	.2
Inhalants	17.4	6.0	2.3	.2
Tranquilizers	14.7	8.0	2.7	.1
Narcotics (Other than heroin)	10.1	5.9	2.1	.1
Heroin	1.1	.5	.2	.0

NA = Figure not available.
Source: *Student Drug Use in America, 1975-81*, a publication of the Institute for Social Research, University of Michigan, and the National Institute on Drug Abuse.

The table above lists drugs more or less in their order of popularity among the class of 1981. Keep in mind that the survey of high school seniors probably underestimates actual drug use among adolescents since it excludes dropouts and truants. Both of these groups have higher rates of drug use than students who regularly attend school. It's also possible that some students are reluctant to admit the extent of their drug use. The survey doesn't measure the overall intake of the fairly large number of kids who mix drugs, or point out at all clearly the drugs that menace younger children. (For example, social scientists read the sharp drop that shows up between the "ever used" and "used in past month" columns under inhalants to mean that some inhalants are used mostly by kids at early ages. I would have missed that.) Chapters four through six contain more detailed information about specific drugs.

THE POLYDRUG PROBLEM

"Polydrugs" is a new word that has sprung up to describe a troublesome new problem: the use of two or more drugs in combination. The drugs may be used either simultaneously or separately during the same general time period. Most of the information we have about polydrugs comes from kids with problems serious enough to bring them to drug clinics or treatment centers. All indications are, however, that polydrug use is high even among "normal" young people.

The two drugs used simultaneously most often are alcohol and marijuana. The chances are almost 100 percent that a young person who smokes marijuana will also have used alcohol. Almost three-fourths of the seniors who use marijuana have mixed it with alcohol, and a large number of this group have used at least one additional illicit drug at some time.

Among kids who end up at drug treatment centers or clinics, polydrug problems are in the majority. One national study reported that more than 80 percent of young people in treatment were involved in some kind of multiple drug abuse. The typical drug abuser in treatment had used three or four different drugs regularly.

Multiple drug use brings multiple problems. Many drugs are lethal at lower levels when they're combined with alcohol, and polydrugs are involved in a third of all drug deaths. There is also evidence that as each new drug is added to a polydrug combination, the risks multiply. That is, each additional drug brings at least two additional medical, social, legal, and/or psychological problems. These problems are especially treacherous because they're unpredictable. The many possible combinations of drugs are complicated by the different physical and psychological makeups of the people who use them. All of these variables make multiple drug use a dangerous gamble. Polydrug users are playing polyroulette — with a wheel that can stop at any number of misfortunes on a single spin.

THE SYMPTOMS OF DRUG ABUSE

Parents often fail to recognize drug problems. No doubt part of the reason for our blindness is that we don't want to see; but it's also true we aren't sure what to look for. The symptoms of drug abuse are not as obvious as those of measles or the flu. Nor are they as definite: none of the clues parents should be aware of is ironclad proof of drug abuse.

If you run across a zip-lock bag of dry, crumbled leaves that look like oregano, chances are you've found marijuana. Other evidence of marijuana smoking includes cigarette papers and the tiny stems and seeds that are discarded. You also may find paraphernalia such as decorative or surgical tweezers (roach clips), soft plastic squeeze bottles (power hitters), or hard plastic cylinders with little spouts and single round holes the size of a fingertip (bongs). Marijuana smoke has a heavy, sweet smell that is easy to detect once you recognize it. People who smoke marijuana may have red eyes and, after a while, respiratory problems. They also may be abnormally hungry, seem listless, and have trouble concentrating.

Serious drug problems almost always bring changes in behavior. Suddenly falling grades, suspensions, or other indications of trouble at school are important clues, particularly in students who have not had previous problems.

Drug abusers may withdraw from the family, spending an unusual amount of time alone in their rooms or away from home. They may not want to go on outings or vacations, or even sit down to eat with the family. They may, in fact, stop eating meals and become careless about their clothing and personal hygiene. On the other hand, they may become unusually fastidious, if that is the norm among their friends. Any striking change may be significant.

Since drug users stick together, young people who have begun heavy drug use often seem to have a whole new circle of friends. They may be vague about who their friends are and what they do together. They probably won't want their parents to meet their new drug-oriented friends.

Personality changes vary. Drug abusers may be irritable and impatient, restless or overactive, or lethargic, depending on the drugs they're taking. They may seem drunk when there is no evidence of alcohol.

Heavy users of drugs often have financial problems, since drugs are expensive. Even those with paper routes or jobs may frequently be broke and need to borrow money, for reasons that may not sound entirely likely. Money or items like cameras and radios that are easily converted to money may suddenly be missing.

Physical evidence of drug use or abuse includes supplies of tablets, capsules, or cough medicine that you know were not prescribed by a doctor. Medicine may be missing from the medicine cabinet. You also might find unexplained large supplies of aerosol products or glue, along with glue-stained plastic bags, rags, or handkerchiefs. People who are injecting drugs may wear long sleeves at unlikely times and places to cover needle marks. They also may have supplies of hypodermic needles, eye droppers, bent spoons, and cotton balls. Users of stimulants and hallucinogens often have dilated pupils that they may hide behind sunglasses. Pinpoint pupils, on the other hand, could be a symptom of narcotic use.

Remember that few of these clues are foolproof. Young people who don't go near drugs are sometimes moody and listless. Red eyes may be caused by simple lack of sleep, and loss of appetite may result from romantic problems.

Since most of the indications of drug abuse can have other causes, parents who detect them should proceed with caution. It's important neither to overreact nor to ignore suspicious symptoms. Don't pounce on your children and accuse them of being junkies. Do keep your eyes and all lines of communication open. If the symptoms you notice include sudden personal changes (appearance, energy, behavior, and so on), arrange a physical examination to check out the possibility of illness before you look for drug use.

Deal with evidence of drug use firmly and immediately. Stay as calm as you can. Try to express your concern without threatening or accusing your children. Be careful not to convey rejection to a child who may desperately need help. Let your kids know that you suspect drug involvement, that you love them, and that they can count on your help to solve any problem. If you have the slightest doubt about your ability to deal with the situation, use the information in chapter eight to locate help.

PROFILE OF A YOUNG DRUG USER

There are at least two roads to understanding what sort of youngster gets involved with drugs. The first is to look at the many research studies carried out during the seventies; the other is to listen to what the kids themselves say. In both cases, a word of caution is in order. Because there have been so many studies with similar results, it's possible to describe in detail the young person *most likely* to use drugs. But that doesn't mean that everyone who fits the description will use drugs, or that everyone who uses drugs will fit the description. There is no need (and certainly no advantage) to panic if the kids in your care seem to be prime candidates, and no reason to relax if they don't. The fact is that all kinds of kids use drugs. As for young peoples' own explanations of their drug use, it's important to remember that few of us at any age understand exactly why we do what we do.

Research studies and surveys have, first of all, come up with some general information that is interesting, but not terribly useful in predicting the danger to any particular young person. For whatever it's worth, within the high-risk age-group (twelve to twenty-five), boys are more likely to use drugs than girls. The risk is also somewhat greater among those who are white, do not have college plans, and live in a large Northeastern city. But all of these differences are small, most are narrowing, and there are exceptions. Girls use more stimulants than boys, for example, and western youngsters use the most cocaine.

Far more important than sex, race, geography, or education is whether kids are influenced more by their parents or peers — a fact that many parents will consider bad news. For parents who don't, here is some revealing information: adolescents' drug use has a close statistical relationship to their friends' approval and practically none to their parents'. Most of the 66 percent of high school seniors who have used drugs believe their parents disapprove of even the most casual drug use.

The single most important factor in beginning to use drugs is the influence of a close friend or friends. This relationship holds at every rung of the drug ladder, from merely experimenting to abusing polydrugs. In addition to recruitment, friends provide role models, information, approval, and moral support. Friends are also part of the marketing system that makes drugs available to teenagers. Kids who get involved with drugs often break ties with their old friends and find new ones who approve and reinforce their habit. Drug users generally spend more time with their friends than other young people, and they go out more often in the evening for recreation.

Parents as a rule don't have a great deal of influence on whether young people experiment with marijuana. If their friends smoke pot, most kids will at least try it. In all other drug use, however, the family is important. How close they are to their parents is almost as influential as friendship when young people decide whether to use illicit drugs other than marijuana.

Serious drug problems often occur in families with other serious problems — violence, alcoholism, poor parent/child or parent/parent relationships. Kids with psychological problems, which usually involve the family, are especially vulnerable. For most parents, however, it may be more important to know that healthy families also can contribute to drug problems. They can do so at the outset by failing to make children clearly understand what sort of behavior is expected of them. Parents can also contribute to problems, once they've begun, by refusing to face them or by shielding their children from the consequences of drug involvement. Parents who find themselves protesting when their youngster is kicked off the team for drug possession, or making up acceptable excuses for school absences when they suspect an illness is drug-related, should take a hard look at their behavior. In the name of protection, they may well be supporting their child's drug abuse.

A number of attempts have been made to learn the secrets of drug-free families. The parents whose kids do not get into drug trouble may have different styles of child rearing, but they have one common feature: close, caring relationships with their children. Drug-free families communicate clearly, cooperate with each other, and are warm and supportive. That doesn't mean, of course, that they never argue. They may disagree vigorously and often, but they can do so without damaging each other or the fabric of the family.

The parents in drug-free families generally are better able than others to prepare children for adult life (see chapter seven), and are satisfied with the way their kids are "turning out." They also like their children's friends. The families enjoy each other, have a strong sense of family tradition, and are efficient at solving problems. Parents have more influence than peers, and both parents and peers express less approval of drug use.

The surveys don't agree about the degree of authority exercised by the parents of drug-free children. One researcher describes such parents as "benevolent dictators." Another reports finding that drug-free families function somewhat democratically. But all seem to agree that, whatever form it comes in, these parents give their children a great deal of guidance, mixed with closeness and support. There is some evidence that drug risk is increased by extremes (whether permissive or authoritarian) of parenting. The families whose children are most likely to have serious problems of all kinds are those whose parents are not involved or interested in them — or those whose parents' interest comes and goes unreliably.

In addition to friendship and parental influence, heavy drug users contrast with nonusers on a long list of personal characteristics and attitudes. High school drug users are likely to have lower grades and less interest in academic achievement than nonusers, though they're often as intelligent. They also tend to be politically liberal, rebellious, impulsive, and critical of society. They place a particularly high value on personal independence. Drug users are less likely to be described either by themselves or their friends in terms of the traditional American values of hard work, ambition, self-reliance, trustworthiness, and capability. On the other hand, high school drug users have some valued characteristics: they score high in creativity, spontaneity, sociability, openness to experience, and interest in the arts, humanities, and social sciences.

Children who get into other kinds of trouble at early

ages have a high probability of getting into drugs. The problems that apply include early drinking and smoking, early sexual experience, trouble with teachers, poor grades, truancy, lying, cheating, fighting, delinquency, and others. The earlier children get into trouble and the more different kinds of trouble they get into, the more likely they are to have serious drug problems. On the other hand, youngsters whose drug taking is limited to occasional marijuana use often have had few or even no early behavior problems.

The explanations of drug use the kids themselves give differ somewhat from those of the experts. The reason young people mention most often in connection with virtually every drug is "to feel good or get high." The rationale mentioned second most often, "to experiment — to see what it's like," obviously applies mostly to first-time users. Experimentation ranks high as a motive for using all drugs and is the number one reason given for using LSD.

Only a small percentage of youngsters directly acknowledge the role of peer pressure that researchers have found so important, although a large number hint at it when they say they use drugs in order to have a good time with their friends. The students I talked with were much more willing than those of the national high school survey to admit peer influence. "Friends" was the word I heard most often. (In suburban schools, incidentally, "parties" was second.) A sizable minority of all students and a larger number of those with serious problems admit using drugs to escape problems or to cope with boredom, anger, and frustration.

Some drugs have special functions. It is not surprising that the first and second reasons given for using stimulants are to increase energy and to stay awake. Barbiturates, tranquilizers, and narcotics are used to relax or relieve tension, to get to sleep, and to relieve pain. Marijuana is also used to relax and relieve tension, and cocaine is thought to have both up and down functions — students give it credit for relieving tension as well as increasing energy. Half of those who use heroin say they do so because of anger and frustration. In addition to their special uses, all of these drugs are also taken to "feel good or get high."

There are a number of areas of agreement between kids and researchers. Both paint complicated pictures. Both stress the importance of friends, although researchers tend to speak about influence and students about sociability. Both mention psychological problems.

Even the differences expressed by young people and social scientists may have threads in common. Researchers say a warm, cohesive family is a strong deterrent to drug use; kids say they use drugs to feel good. My theory is that young people with strong family relationships feel good in the first place. They're also less vulnerable to peer pressure, and less likely to need drugs to relieve psychological distress.

Parents can help children feel good without drugs by encouraging their interests, constructive activities, and achievements. Kids who have goals *of their own that are attainable*, and thus feel successful, don't need drugs to feel good. They've experienced a high that is much better in the long run: feeling good about themselves.

Of course, no child-rearing system is foolproof. Outside pressures are enormous, and the children of model parents sometimes get involved with drugs. The point is that kids raised in warm, supportive families with clear communication and a lot of guidance are better equipped to face outside pressure of all kinds. They're even better fortified if they've learned to make decisions and accept responsibility.

No one who has tried it would suggest building a warm, strong family is easy. But thousands of former children would testify that it can be done. The beauty is it's one door parents can open: strengthening the family is the one deterrent to drug use parents are directly in position to provide.

Chapter Four

Alcohol and tobacco

Alcohol and tobacco are the "licit" drugs, not only legal but respectable for adults in much of our society. Billboards, magazine ads, and TV commercials bombard us and our children with the notion that these social chemicals are used by beautiful, successful, sexy people. Many of us enjoy — or can't stop using — them ourselves. We urge drinks on our guests as a mark of hospitality. We chuckle as comedians do drunk routines. We teach our kids by example that alcohol is the starter fluid that gets a party going. We may even tell them that we "need" a drink after a harried day.

Young people have bought the media's message and (for once) have learned what we've been teaching. They use and abuse more alcohol than any other drug in their repertoire. More of them pollute their lungs with tobacco than with marijuana.

Both alcohol and tobacco have long-term health consequences at least as serious as any of the illicit drugs we're so much in fear of. Alcohol is also dangerous in the short run. Our concern to protect our kids from exotic new perils is justified, but we ought not to overlook old familiar dangers that are just as deadly. We may need to reevaluate our definition of a dangerous drug.

ALCOHOL

Drinking is an American tradition. The Pilgrims drank "bere" on the Mayflower and we have been at it ever since. While we would prefer not to see our children plastered, many of us expect them to use alcoholic beverages when or even as they grow up. Drinking is not only accepted but expected in many segments of society. We don't regard alcohol with the fear and outrage that we do other drugs.

The irony for youth and adults alike is that alcohol has created more havoc in our society than all other drugs put together. For one thing, it has had a longer time to do so. For another, right up to the present moment, it remains the most used recreational drug in America, even among children and adolescents. The figures that follow should convince most of us that alcohol is our number one adolescent drug problem:

● More than 70 percent of the nation's high school seniors had used alcohol during the month before the 1981 survey (32 percent had used marijuana).

● More than half of the senior boys and about 30 percent of the senior girls had been drunk (that is, had had five or more drinks in a row) during the two weeks before the 1980 survey.

● Alcohol-related accidents are the leading cause of death among fifteen to twenty-four-year-olds.

● A fifth of our twelve and thirteen-year-olds are current drinkers.

The quantity that kids drink at a sitting may be a better measure of the problem than how often they drink. Binge drinking has become an adolescent custom. The number of drinks per drinking occasion is highest among sixteen and seventeen-year- olds—the age-group that includes our youngest and least experienced drivers.

The Adolescent Drinker. As a group, young drinkers fit into the profile of drug users described in the preceding chapter. That is, they are likely (but far from certain)

32

to be boys, have low academic goals, place high value on personal independence, and so on. Like most drug users, they are heavily influenced by their friends. The most common drinking situation for high school seniors is a party. Few youngsters drink alone, although those who do drink heavily.

Adolescent drinking is also related to how much kids believe their parents drink. Teenage teetotalers are more likely to report having parents who are also teetotalers and/or who disapprove of teenage drinking. Young people who belong to fundamentalist religious groups have especially low drinking rates.

The U.S. Secretary of Health and Human Services recently reported that teenage problem drinkers (those who are drunk at least once a week) differ from other teenagers in some important aspects:

● They are relatively more influenced by their friends than their parents.

● They are more likely to have friends who are problem drinkers and who approve their drinking.

● They experience more conflict between the values of their friends and those of their parents.

● Their parents are less involved in their lives.

● Their parents themselves are heavier drinkers.

● Their parents are less likely to disapprove their drinking.

● Their parents give them less support and affection.

The History of Alcohol. Alcohol has been around for a long time. By the time historians appeared on the human scene, it had already become part of the world's rituals, food supply, and recreation. In some cultures, one of which is our own, excessive use has been a problem.

In this country, alcohol was a staple from the beginning. Every frontier settlement had its brewer of beer or its distiller of corn whiskey. Drunkenness became enough of a problem to inspire the temperance movement that led to Prohibition. During that period, bootleggers enjoyed the same sort of financial bonanza that drug smugglers exploit today. During Prohibition, drinking in this country first declined and then soared, as the underground market became established. After repeal, we continued on our course as one of those cultures that both uses and abuses alcohol. Today, the use of alcohol is so common in our society that not drinking is somewhat like refusing to ride in automobiles — it requires a deliberate decision.

The Chemistry and Effects of Alcohol. Alcohol can more than hold its own among other drugs in terms of negative effects. Its active ingredient is ethyl alcohol, a drug that depresses the central nervous system. (Ironically, many people become stimulated and some become aggressive when they've been drinking. These effects result from loss of inhibition.)

SHORT-TERM EFFECTS. In small amounts, alcohol acts as a mild and often pleasant tranquilizer; in large amounts, it is disastrous. The amount a person can drink safely varies with age, sex, weight, mood, health, drinking experience, and food intake, among other factors.

When the blood contains more than .10 percent alcohol (a condition that requires only four cans of beer in an hour by a 150-pound boy), the drinker's memory, muscle coordination, and reaction time are affected. He has become a dangerous driver and, in most states, has reached the legal threshold of intoxication.

With larger amounts, the senses are severely dulled, judgment is affected, and the person may become either aggressive or depressed. At .30 percent blood alcohol level (BAL), a point that can be reached by an inexperienced hundred-pound girl with little more than a six-pack, the drinker reaches the point of drunken stupor with no comprehension of what is going on around her. At .40 percent BAL, the drinker may well be dead. The lethal level is lower when alcohol is combined (as it often is among adolescents) with barbiturates, Quaaludes, or other downer drugs.

ACCIDENTS, VIOLENCE, AND DEATH. Alcohol-related accidents are the leading cause of death among teenagers, and drinking is a factor in half of our country's traffic deaths. (A recent study indicates the relationship between alcohol and traffic fatalities may be underestimated. Blood samples of 600 drivers killed in single-car accidents in North Carolina from 1978-81 revealed that 79 percent had been drinking and more than 67 percent were legally intoxicated.) Alcohol is involved in many of the teenage suicides that now account for one of every ten deaths within the age-group. Drinking also contributes to murder, industrial accidents, falls, burns, and drownings.

LONG-TERM HEALTH EFFECTS. The health hazards associated with heavy drinking would fill a dictionary of diseases. One of the most serious is cirrhosis of the liver, the fourth leading cause of death among American adults (ages 24-64). Abusive drinking leads to several diseases of the heart, and increases the risk of cancer of the tongue, mouth, throat, esophagus, larynx, and liver. It is related to high blood pressure, stroke, phlebitis, and other ailments. Chronic heavy drinkers are likely to have damage to the brain and nervous system.

BIRTH DEFECTS. The condition called "fetal alcohol syndrome" (FAS) is especially important to teenagers since so many of them are having babies. There is now extensive evidence that drinking during pregnancy may result in a cluster of birth defects including mental retardation, poor motor ability, growth deficiencies, and abnormalities of the face.

SOCIAL, LEGAL, AND ECONOMIC EFFECTS. Heavy drinking contributes to family problems, including child and spouse abuse, unwanted pregnancy, loss of income, drunk driving charges, and countless other problems. The most serious cost to young people is probably interrupted development. Kids who are regularly drunk (like those who are stoned) may not develop the personal, social, and professional skills they need to function as adults.

Trouble Signs. There is a fuzzy line between "problem drinking" and alcoholism. Roughly speaking, people become problem drinkers when their drinking begins to cause trouble for themselves, their families, or their associates. The symptoms may be frequent drunkenness, arrests for drunk driving, family problems, absences from school, and so on. The National Council on Alcoholism defines alcoholism as "a disease in which the use of alcohol interferes with health, social, and economic functioning." Usually, alcoholics are unable to control their drinking.

What You Can Do. The first thing you can do about alcohol is to recognize it is a drug, every bit as dangerous to youngsters as the illicit drug you're most afraid of. The next step is to review your own stand on drinking — that is, whether you have opted for abstinence or moderation for yourself and your children. Remember that, either way, you and they will have to maintain the position in the midst of a drinking society.

URGING ABSTINENCE. There is a lot to be said for abstinence. Teetotalers never become alcoholics, and the children of abstainers also often abstain. But don't expect your kids to abstain if you don't. On the other hand, if you're a teetotaler, be careful not to turn off your children by appearing to be judgmental or self-righteous. Remember that they know a lot of fine people who drink. If your kids decide to drink against your wishes, they'll probably try to do it without your knowledge, making it more difficult for you to help them. It's important to take a calm, rational position against drinking, to be sure your kids understand your position and the reasons for it, and to stay in close communication.

TEACHING MODERATE USE. For those who decide to help their kids learn to drink responsibly, there are some lessons to be learned from cultures in which people drink but rarely have drinking problems. Societies — and families — who drink "successfully" tend to be especially close-knit. They have a firm tradition of moderate drinking and strong social sanctions against drunkenness, which is not considered comic. Otherwise, though, alcohol is not a major issue — it is not thought to be especially good, evil, or important. Most drinking takes place at meals, in rituals, or in other special situations. It is not viewed as an indication of adulthood, or used as a device for coping or escape. Drinking is a matter of choice—no one pushes drinks or makes a fuss if a guest or family member decides not to have one.

If kids are to drink responsibly, they need ground rules and some information. They need to know when, where, and how much they can drink with your approval. Your position will presumably be in line with your state's drinking laws, which both you and your children will need to know. Young people also need to understand their own physiological drinking limits. The chart below, showing average effects of drinking in relation to body weight, is a good place to begin understanding limits. Be sure, though, that your youngsters also know that their alcohol safety levels are affected by other factors: sex (girls ordinarily can't drink as much as boys with safety), whether or not they've eaten, their health, the use of carbonated mixes, and others.

You'll also need to establish rules for driving and drinking: what do your children do, for example, when the driver of the car they've been riding in has been overdrinking? (Some counselors recommend a contract in which kids agree never to ride with a driver who's been drinking and parents agree to pick up children who get stranded at any hour.) For help with these and other issues, write to the National Clearinghouse for Alcohol Information (address at the end of chapter eight) for the following pamphlets: "How to Talk With Your Teenager About Driving and Drinking;" "The Drinking Question: Honest Answers to Questions Teenagers Ask About Drinking;" and "Drinking Etiquette." One copy of each pamphlet will be sent to you free.

AVERAGE EFFECTS OF DRINKING

Body Weight	Drinks Two-Hour Period 1½ ozs. 86 Proof Liquor or 12 ozs. Beer											
100	1	2	3	4	5	6	7	8	9	10	11	12
120	1	2	3	4	5	6	7	8	9	10	11	12
140	1	2	3	4	5	6	7	8	9	10	11	12
160	1	2	3	4	5	6	7	8	9	10	11	12
180	1	2	3	4	5	6	7	8	9	10	11	12
200	1	2	3	4	5	6	7	8	9	10	11	12
220	1	2	3	4	5	6	7	8	9	10	11	12
240	1	2	3	4	5	6	7	8	9	10	11	12

Reasonable	**Unsafe**	**Illegal**
Be careful	Driving Impaired	Do Not Drive
Blood Alcohol	Blood Alcohol	Blood Alcohol
Content	Content	Content
.00 to .05	.05 — .09	.10 & Up

Source: National Highway Traffic Safety Administration.

GETTING HELP WHEN IT'S NEEDED. If a member of your family shows signs of a developing drinking problem, your best bet is professional help. The recovery rate *for those who get treatment* is high. Clinics, hospitals, and other agencies that treat drinking problems are listed in the yellow pages of my phone book under "Alcoholism Information and Treatment Centers." Before you let your fingers start walking, however, you may want to read the section on drug and alcohol treatment centers in chapter eight.

You also need to know that people with drinking problems often staunchly resist the idea that they need help. If the drinker is a minor, you may need to insist that he or she get treatment, preferably involving the family. In the meantime, there are some other ways you can help. First, learn everything you can about drinking and alcoholism. Books and pamphlets are widely available, and many alcoholism counselors will be happy to give you information firsthand. Next, take a hard look at your own behavior to be sure that, without intending to, you aren't supporting the drinking problem (by making excuses for the drinker, for example, or by lending money). You can also help your child become aware of the problem by calmly describing his or her specific behavior in a nonjudgmental way *when he or she is sober.* That is, you can say "Your friend had to bring you home because you passed out at the party last night," but not "Your mother and I were embarrassed to death by your outrageous behavior."

Probably most important, you can get counseling and support for yourself through alcohol information agencies, mental health clinics, and organizations like Alcoholics Anonymous and Al-Anon Family Groups. AA is intended first and foremost for alcoholics themselves, but is often willing to help families. The members of Al-Anon are people whose spouses, children, other relatives, or friends have drinking problems. They meet to support each other and to work out problems that arise in their own lives as a result of the drinking of a family member or friend. In the process, although Al-Anon cannot show how to stop someone else's drinking, members learn new attitudes that may encourage the drinker to get treatment sooner. At the very least, they learn not to hinder the solution of a drinking problem. Alateen is a part of Al-Anon for teenagers whose family members or friends are problem drinkers. The addresses of the national headquarters of both Alcoholics Anonymous and Al-Anon Family Groups (for those who may want to locate or start a group) are listed at the end of chapter eight.

TOBACCO

Tobacco is the one recreational drug that can be taken without a lot of hassle almost anywhere. It's perfectly respectable to give yourself a nicotine fix on Main Street. More than 50,000,000 Americans take advantage of this tolerance to light up regularly.

Americans of all ages are well aware of the dangers of smoking. They know that cigarettes are deadly in the long run. Still, millions of otherwise sensible people go on abusing their bodies with tobacco. The question that shouts itself from the hilltops is "Why?" One of the answers is that it's hard to stop — cigarettes are extremely addictive.

The addictive chemical, among the fifty or so ingredients of tobacco, appears to be nicotine. The cigarette is a highly efficient apparatus that rushes the drug to the brain, puff-upon-puff, faster than mainlined heroin. Each cigarette is capable of ten doses, and it's estimated that the pack-a-day smoker gets 70,000 "hits" per year.

Young people may begin smoking because of peer pressure or because it makes them feel grown up and sophisticated or satisfies a need to rebel, but they continue because they get hooked. One research study turned up the startling statistic that 85 percent of the kids who experiment with smoking will become regular dependent smokers. Once they're addicted, it's very difficult for most people to stop smoking.

The Young Smoker. Anyone who ventured into a high school restroom during the early seventies is probably a candidate for lung cancer. By comparison, the smoke-filled rooms that politicians are supposed to meet in are havens of fresh air. Teenage smoking reached its peak around 1974, when a quarter of the age-group classified themselves as current smokers.

Until the 1970s, most hard-core adolescent smokers had been boys. In 1968, twice as many boys as girls reported current smoking. But during the following decade, girls not only caught up with but went beyond their brothers and boyfriends.

Today, like all Americans, young people of both sexes are cutting back on smoking. Currently, 10 to 12 percent (less than half of the 1974 rate) of those in the twelve to seventeen age-group are regular smokers. Since smoking is related to age, the figures for upper classmen are higher. Still, the 21.3 percent of high school seniors who reported daily smoking in 1980 represented a decrease of four percent in just one year. The 1981 decrease was smaller (one percent).

These figures are heartening. But statistics are small comfort to the parent whose child risks disease and death by getting hooked on smoking. Children who begin smoking early are more likely to become the lifelong smokers who take the greatest health risk. Early smokers are also prone to use alcohol and other drugs, and to have other behavior problems. I'd recommend doing anything you can to prevent, or at least delay, this habit in your children.

There are some interesting relationships between teenagers who smoke and their families. Teenagers from single-parent homes are about twice as likely to be smokers than others. Kids from two-parent homes are also at high risk if both parents smoke. Teenagers are about three times more likely to smoke if an older brother or sister smokes. Taken together, these relationships are strong. The teenager who lives in a traditional household where no other member smokes is highly unlikely to become a smoker.

As in all drug-related behavior, friends are important. Smokers tend to have friends who smoke, and nonsmokers to have friends who don't. With the unexplained exception of boys in the fifteen to sixteen age-group, young people who are employed are more likely to smoke than others. Smokers also tend to come from the ranks of those who aren't highly motivated, successful in school, nor headed for college.

The History of Tobacco. When Europeans came to the New World, one of their first acts was to exchange drugs with the natives. The Indians introduced the explorers to tobacco, of which they had the total world supply. In return, the original Americans got alcohol. In terms of trouble, it was a fair exchange.

By the beginning of the seventeenth century, tobacco had become an important cash crop in Virginia. The economic importance of tobacco forms one horn of the dilemma our government is currently hung up on—funding anti-smoking campaigns at the same time that it subsidizes the production of tobacco.

Cigarettes, which seem to be the most harmful form of tobacco, became popular in this country after 1880. Per-capita cigarette use and deaths from lung cancer rose together at the same rapid rate during the sixty-year period after 1900.

In 1964, the Surgeon General of the United States first reported that cigarettes are hazardous to health. Since that time, smoking in America has declined, although not enough to threaten the cigarette industry or significantly improve public health. Most modern cigarettes contain less tar and nicotine than those of the pre-1960 era, and many are filtered. It's often said that today's toughest tonsils would choke on a Camel or Lucky Strike from the 1950s.

The Chemistry and Effects of Tobacco. The three ingredients of tobacco known to be important are nicotine, tar, and carbon monoxide. Nicotine is extremely toxic. The nausea and dizziness felt by beginning smokers is caused by low-level nicotine poisoning, which the body eventually adapts to. Nicotine is also the source of the effects (relaxation, stimulation, pleasure) that are enticing. The carbon monoxide in tobacco smoke appears to be the villain in cigarette-caused heart attack and stroke. Tar, on the other hand, carries the cancer-causing compounds.

SHORT-TERM EFFECTS. Tobacco is a stimulant that also appears to have relaxing qualities, although some researchers believe it relaxes only by relieving the withdrawal stress that sets in after a period of not smoking. Tobacco also provides pleasure, whether as a result of some chemical on the brain's pleasure center or through some more subtle psychological device. It involves the mouth, which is the center of our earliest and most enduring pleasures.

One of the most seductive features of smoking, especially for young people, is the lack of immediate ill effects. Aside from bad breath and the disfavor of nonsmokers, the only problems likely to show up during the first few years of smoking are higher rates of bronchitis and other respiratory ailments. Unlike other drugs, tobacco does not reduce the user's ability to function. It may, in fact, improve it. All of the bad consequences are far away in a future that is inconceivable to strong, healthy adolescents. To them, old age and ill health are handicaps distributed in a lottery they had the good sense not to enter.

LONG-TERM HEALTH EFFECTS. The Surgeon General calls cigarette smoking "the largest single preventable cause of illness and premature death" in the United States today. Cigarette smokers have a 70 percent greater rate of early death than nonsmokers.

The largest number of smoking-related deaths results from cardiovascular ailments. Nearly twice as many smokers as nonsmokers die annually from heart disease. Smoking also often leads to stroke, clogged coronary arteries, circulatory problems of the arms and legs, and rupture of the aorta. The combination of birth control pills and smoking greatly increases the risk of heart attack and stroke in women. Some of these effects are reversible. An ex-smoker's risk of heart disease, for example, is considerably lower after two years of not smoking and may disappear altogether after a decade.

Cigarette smoking causes more deaths from cancer than any other presently known agent. Ninety percent of all lung cancer occurs among smokers. At the present rate of increase, lung cancer will become the leading cause of cancer death among women during the 1980s. Smokers also run a greater risk of ulcers and cancer of the mouth, larynx, esophagus, bladder, and pancreas.

DANGERS IN REPRODUCTION. The dangers of smoking to reproduction are especially important to teenagers as their pregnancy rates climb. The risks of premature birth, stillbirth, and newborn death are higher than normal among the babies of smoking mothers. The risk of miscarriage may be as much as 80 percent higher among smokers. The babies of smokers tend to have lower birth weights, making them especially vulnerable to illness and death in infancy.

What You Can Do. If you are a smoker, probably the best way you can protect your children from the dangers of smoking is to stop smoking. If your children smoke, promote a family kick-the-habit project. Self-quit kits are available from the American Cancer Society, and many hospitals and clinics offer stop-smoking programs. From all reports, you won't find stopping easy, but you'll be giving both yourself and your children the gift of health in the future.

THE ROLE OF INFORMATION. The hazards of smoking have been pretty well communicated by school health classes. There is some controversy about whether knowing the risks has much effect on adolescent smoking. It may be that young people are cutting down because smoking isn't as socially acceptable as it once was. Still, all of us should make sure our children are aware of the dangers, without resorting to scare tactics or expecting kids to be very worried about such a distant health threat.

Whether at school or at home, anti-smoking information may be most effective within the larger framework of a general fitness program. All children should realize how easy it is to become addicted, and how difficult to get rid of the addiction. They also should know that, contrary to popular opinion, everyone does *not* do it. Teenagers should be aware that their peers who smoke (currently 10 to 12 percent) are a shrinking minority.

FAMILY PREVENTION. Some of the more successful anti-smoking programs in schools go beyond health information to help kids understand and deal with the pressures that make them want to smoke. As parents, we can conduct similar informal programs at home. We might point out the fresh good looks of the young people in cigarette ads, for example, and suggest that our kids notice how many real-life smokers are as young and attractive.

All of us should become "teaching parents" (for many good purposes beyond discouraging smoking). Without mounting a soapbox, we can talk with our kids about what is going on each time we resist pressure from our peers or the media. We should make sure they understand what we did, why we did it, and how our decision fits into our long-term philosophy. We should congratulate our kids when they make similar decisions. We also can look for opportunities to work through choices, considering both short and long-term consequences, as a family. Finally, we should do everything we can to improve our children's self-concepts, their senses of individuality, and their own abilities to make and stick by decisions.

Chapter Five

Marijuana

When you see it growing, marijuana doesn't look much like a menace. It makes a lovely houseplant that belongs in a setting with wicker furniture, a ceiling fan, and Polynesian sculpture. It's hard to believe that its graceful foliage could cause so much commotion.

Pot, after all, is "organic." Some of its fans refer to it as grass or herb, names that sound downright beneficial. It seemed like madness to the kids of the sixties when they were thrown in jail for using marijuana, which they considered harmless, while their parents slowly pickled themselves with legal martinis. In those days the battle raged —sometimes literally—between folks who thought smoking marijuana was a sign of high sensibility and those who saw it as a dark alien threat, ranking with communism and fluoridated water.

Today, the controversy focuses on the dangers of marijuana to health and adolescent development. The question is no longer *whether* the drug is hazardous (that has been established), but *how* hazardous it is.

The marijuana controversy is examined, item by item, later in this chapter. But this much needs to be said at the outset: *the use of marijuana is not safe for adolescents, not physically or psychologically, or any other way that I'm aware of.* Even the most enthusiastic advocates of marijuana for adults agree that it's bad news for adolescents.

In addition to long-term health problems (both known and suspected), the use of the drug often involves children in drug-oriented peer groups. It can reduce energy and motivation. It interferes with driving ability. Young people who use it are much more likely than others to try other illicit drugs. Perhaps most significant for children, the use of marijuana can seriously interfere with learning and development — the principal business of the adolescent years.

THE SIZE OF THE PROBLEM

When drugs raced through the school system during the 1970s, marijuana led the field. The number of seniors who had tried the drug tripled and daily users increased by an incredible 650 percent during that troubled decade.

Throughout the post-1965 epidemic, marijuana has been by far the most widely used illicit drug. More than 90 percent of those who use drugs have used marijuana. By 1981, 60 percent of graduating seniors had tried it; 32 percent had used it in the month just before the survey; and seven percent used it daily.

Both monthly and daily marijuana smoking among high school seniors began to decrease in 1980. This decline has been widely interpreted to mean that the marijuana epidemic has peaked. But before we get too comfortable, we need to remember that as peaks go, this one is Mount Everest. The seven percent figure in the daily column means that roughly 210,000 boys and girls in the senior class smoke marijuana almost every day. Only a portion of the huge increase that took place during the seventies was undone by the decrease of the early eighties. The important point is that neither marijuana nor drugs in general will stop posing a serious threat to children in any early future.

Why has marijuana smoking become so commonplace among young people? Most of the reasons — the loosening of family and community ties, uncertainty and change, our pill mentality, and others—discussed in chapter two apply to marijuana. Within that framework, the drug has had some particular advantages in the eyes of adolescents. For one thing, it has been readily available. For another, until recently, kids believed that marijuana did not involve a health risk. Probably most important, pot has been widely considered "cool" by young peer groups. It is revealing that as the marijuana tide began to turn in 1980, two of those factors also changed significantly. The proportion of high school seniors who believed using marijuana regularly involved a serious health risk jumped from 35 to 58 percent between 1978-81. At the same time, the percentage reporting that their close friends approved smoking marijuana dropped significantly.

WHO USES MARIJUANA?

By 1979, a majority (68 percent) of Americans under the age of twenty-six had at least tried marijuana. Smoking pot was no longer confined to troublemakers or kids mad at the system. For that matter, it was no longer confined to kids. The use of marijuana by adults had been steadily increasing.

The major users of the drug, however, are young people between the ages of twelve and twenty-five. During the seventies, the rate of increase was largest among twelve to seventeen-year-olds, the group in which the use of drugs is most alarming. Although national statistics suggest that extensive use of the drug begins at the seventh grade, there are persistent reports of youngsters beginning sooner.

Much of the description of a typical drug user reported in chapter three originally came from research among kids who smoked marijuana. But today, with 60 percent of the nation's senior class involved to some degree, marijuana users obviously have many temperaments and backgrounds. Athletes and the inactive, top and bottom scholars, class presidents and clowns, rich kids and poor kids, and those in between have all been known to try marijuana. Unfortunately, it has become one of the rites of initiation into what kids think of as adulthood.

Regular or daily marijuana smokers, on the other hand, still fall neatly into the drug-user profile. They tend to be white males who live in cities and are not headed for college. As a group, they are poorer students, truant more often, less religious, and more liberal politically than other young people. They spend a lot of time away from home looking for fun and recreation. Chances are much higher that they'll use alcohol, other drugs, and tobacco. Although casual marijuana smoking is not related to psychological problems, daily smokers often report using the drug in order to cope with their frustrations.

The one part of the profile that still applies to using marijuana occasionally or experimentally is the influence of friends. Friends are the all-important ingredient in the marijuana muddle. Study after study has shown that the young people most likely to try marijuana are those whose friends are users. Unfortunately, pot-smoking friends are as common as they are influential: 83 percent of the class of 1981 reported having a friend or friends who smoked marijuana.

The role of friends in marijuana smoking goes beyond the peer pressure that applies to dress and dating. Pot is a social drug, used most often in the company of one or two special friends. Young people who are asked if they use drugs often answer, "No ... well, sometimes I smoke with my friends." The reason given second most often (right after "to feel good or get high") for using marijuana is "to have a good time with my friends."

Friends not only introduce the drug, but they give instruction in effective smoking. They also teach the rituals and rules like sharing, which is required by pot etiquette. A joint is prepared in a little ceremony that is informal but rarely varied, and then passed around the room like a peace pipe. The whole procedure has an air of sacrament about it.

According to the statistics, parents don't have a very big influence on the casual use of marijuana. Although a huge majority of the class of 1981 believed that their parents would disapprove of even the most modest use of marijuana, 60 percent had gone ahead and done it. The message in that is you're not a total failure if you catch your youngsters experimenting.

What is far more important than whether kids try marijuana is the next step: whether they satisfy their curiosity and go on to more constructive matters, or get stuck in the pot rut. And parents are extremely important at that intersection. The young people who do not become seriously involved with marijuana (or other drugs, for that matter) tend to have strong, warm relationships with their parents. Their families are able to provide them with clear guidelines and affectionate support. There is a mutual respect and good communication. If you think your family has a problem in some of those areas, your kids may be especially vulnerable to drug problems. If so, I strongly recommend that you look for some help. You may want to try family counseling, take a course in parenting, get some books from the library, or work out your own program for strengthening your family's defenses. The important thing is to do something.

If the situation in your family has gone beyond vulnerability and you think one of your children may have a drug problem, action is even more important. Forget your pride and get treatment. Resources for treating drug problems are now available in or near every community. You'll find some pointers on how to go about locating help in this book's final chapter.

WHAT MARIJUANA IS AND WHERE IT CAME FROM

Marijuana comes from one of the earth's oldest cultivated plants. The scientific term for it is *Cannabis sativa* and its common name is hemp. The plant belongs to the same family as the hemp from which rope used to be made. George Washington grew hemp, and some imaginative souls have interpreted horticultural notes in his diary to mean that the father of our country was actually growing pot on the Potomac. More sober historians, including me, doubt that interpretation.

Dried marijuana, which looks a lot like oregano, is usually smoked but can also be eaten. It contains at least 421 chemicals, many of whose effects are unknown. The drug becomes even more complex as it burns. The principal psychoactive ingredient (that is, the chemical that contributes the most to the drug experience) is Delta-9 tetrahydrocannabinol, or THC. THC occurs in the resin that is found in the plant's flowering tops and, to a lesser extent, in its leaves. In recent years, the most advanced horticultural technology has been applied to produce marijuana with a higher THC content.

Some of the confusion about the drug's safety has to do with potency. Critics point out regularly that many of the studies that seemed to indicate marijuana was harmless were conducted during the early 1970s when the THC content of an average marijuana cigarette was about one percent. By 1979, marijuana sold on the street commonly contained four or five percent THC. Hash or hashish, a resin concentrate made from the flowering tops of the marijuana plant, may contain up to 12 percent THC. A third form, hash oil, made by boiling hashish in a solvent, typically has a 15 to 20 percent THC content, but can be produced to contain more than 60 percent THC. The safety issue is further clouded by the unknown effects of the many other chemicals contained in marijuana.

Hemp has been used as a drug in the eastern world for thousands of years. One of the oldest accounts of its use was written by Herodotus, describing a Scythian wake, about 450 B.C. The father of history didn't fully understand what he was observing; but when we read his description from our vantage point, it's pretty obvious what the Scythians were up to. The first important use of cannabis in the west took place in Paris in the 1840s among a group of artists and literary types who wrote about the experience in detail.

In this country, the drug had a much more mundane introduction. Marijuana apparently first entered the United States by crossing the Mexican border during the early years of this century. About the same time, it also began to come into the port of New Orleans. Early on, marijuana was used extensively by lower-class minority groups in southern cities like New Orleans and El Paso. Because these groups had high crime rates (with or without marijuana), the drug soon was widely reputed to cause violent crime. Eventually, marijuana moved up the Mississippi to other American cities.

By 1936, all forty-eight states had outlawed marijuana. During the late forties, the drug was discovered by the small group of disenchanted intellectuals known as the beatniks, who passed it on to their successors, the hippies and flower children. As the youth culture inspired by these groups spread throughout the country during the sixties, so did the drug. The use of marijuana was also spread by servicemen returning from Vietnam, where drugs were a major problem.

Although marijuana use grew rapidly throughout the sixties, it was more or less confined to hippies, protesters, college kids, servicemen, musicians, and residents of ghettos. Then, during the seventies, it exploded downward to high schools and junior highs, and outward from cities and campuses to towns, suburbs, villages and rural communities. Today, you can find marijuana in the smallest backwoods hamlet.

During the 1970s, eleven states decriminalized possession of the drug—that is, made possession of less than an ounce of marijuana a low-penalty civil (rather than criminal) offense. Four states also decriminalized the transfer of small amounts from person to person when no sale is involved. More recently, the national parent movement has been instrumental in halting the trend toward relaxation of possession penalties. The sale of marijuana is still illegal throughout the country.

THE CONTROVERSY

Marijuana has been the subject of a great deal of confusion and controversy. Some adults, many of whom are parents, view the drug with terror and believe the worst about it. The stereotype example is the couple who say, "Thank God they're not using drugs," when their kids come home in an alcoholic stupor. Young people, on the other hand, have tended to regard all warnings about the dangers of marijuana as scare tactics. Misinformation is plentiful on both sides.

Another problem is the incomplete state of the data. It will be years before many of the long-range effects of marijuana smoking have been scientifically established. Some effects that teachers and drug professionals firmly believe in have not yet been conclusively demonstrated by research. And some of the studies that have been conducted have had conflicting results. Meanwhile, our children are engaged in a dangerous national experiment.

But there are some facts that can be stated with certainty and some probabilities that can be pointed out. Unfortunately, few of them offer much comfort to parents.

Is Marijuana Hazardous to Health? My research revealed no record that anyone has ever died of a marijuana overdose, and people who smoke it don't turn into raving maniacs. The Addiction Research Foundation of Canada goes so far as to report that "an occasional high is probably not physically hazardous unless the user attempts to drive, fly, or operate heavy machinery." Beyond those scant reassurances, though, the health news isn't hopeful.

First, there are some short-term problems. Unpleasant side effects reported by some marijuana users include dulled senses and reflexes, anxiety or panic stemming from a feeling of loss of control, and mild paranoia. Some smokers experience more severe psychological reactions that may involve delusions, hallucinations, and retreat from reality. A few people also experience flashbacks (repetition of unpleasant symptoms days or weeks after they originally occur). Flashbacks occur most frequently among marijuana users who have also used LSD.

Most people experience an increased heart rate soon after using marijuana. This condition is apparently not dangerous to those in good health, but can bring on chest pain (angina) in people with a poor blood supply to the heart. There is also clear evidence that THC and other ingredients of pot enter the bloodstream of an unborn child. While the exact effects are not known, pregnant women obviously should avoid marijuana along with all other unnecessary drugs.

Other problems may result from impurities in street marijuana, which is processed and marketed by some pretty unscrupulous people. In recent years, there have been a number of cases in which young people have unknowingly smoked marijuana laced with more dangerous substances such as the drug, PCP.

There is now convincing evidence that, in the long run, smoking marijuana will prove to be more dangerous than smoking tobacco. Heavy smokers currently suffer higher than normal rates of sore throat, laryngitis, bronchitis, and other respiratory problems. In the future, according to a growing body of evidence, they are likely to be candidates for cancer. Chronic heavy smoking of marijuana causes inflammation and pretumorous conditions in the airways much like those produced by smoking tobacco. In addition, marijuana smoke contains almost as much carbon monoxide as tobacco smoke and considerably larger amounts of two tars known to be cancer-producing. The problem is compounded by the chemical complexity of marijuana and by the way it is smoked: the smoke is inhaled more deeply and held in the lungs longer than tobacco smoke, and the unfiltered tar-rich butt is usually consumed.

There is also evidence that marijuana affects hormone

production, lowers fertility in both men and women, decreases resistance to infection, affects cell membranes and enzymes, alters chromosome distribution during cell division, and causes some changes in brain structure and function. The effects on hormones and the reproductive system are especially worrisome for adolescents, whose bodies are rapidly growing and developing. It's true that some of these problems have yet to be conclusively demonstrated to the satisfaction of scientists but, if you're like me, you probably don't want your kids to be the guinea pigs.

If logic is any indication, the long-term effects of marijuana will turn out to be intensified by the drug's long "staying power." Traces of a single dose of marijuana may remain in the body for thirty days or longer. Moreover, marijuana is "fat soluble," a characteristic that in other drugs leads to storage in body tissues, including the brain. These two facts, taken together, mean that repeated use of even small amounts of pot may lead to a high accumulation of the drug in the body, and that the bodies of regular heavy smokers are exposed to large accumulations over long time periods. The complexity of the drug at best adds to the uncertainty and at worse to the danger.

Does Marijuana Interfere with Learning and Development? This question could hardly be more important when we're talking about adolescent children; and clear evidence tells us the answer is an emphatic yes. Research has demonstrated that a wide range of mental abilities including thought, speech, reading comprehension, attention span, problem solving, and others are lower during marijuana intoxication. Most of the lowered abilities stem from temporary damage to long-term memory. Ill effects can result from a single moderate dose.

The result in the classroom is that students have trouble learning when they're high on marijuana. It's certain that regular smokers miss out on a lot of education. The problem is aggravated by the fact that smoking at school is common. A recent statewide New York study, for example, found that half of all current marijuana users had been high at least once in class.

The effect of heavy use on psychological development is much more difficult to demonstrate in the research lab. For one thing, no one wants to subject kids deliberately to heavy use of marijuana, even in the interest of science. But the evidence we have indicates that young people who are regularly stoned fail to develop the skills in personal problem solving, coping, decision making, and social interacteraction that are ordinarily learned through trial and error during the adolescent years. Adulthood is likely to be difficult for people who use marijuana as a security blanket during adolescence.

Does Marijuana Interfere with Driving Ability? Researchers report that marijuana hinders driving ability by interfering with motor coordination, concentration, and judgment. It also significantly reduces the ability to follow a moving object (tracking) and distorts the user's sense of time and space. These conclusions come from studies using driving simulators and test courses.

Young people, on the other hand, often insist they're better drivers when they've smoked marijuana because they "get into" their driving and are less impatient. Unfortunately the evidence on the other side is clear and consistent. The combination of alcohol and marijuana (a common phenomenon in the age-group) is particularly dangerous on the highway.

Tests to measure the marijuana intoxication of drivers are expected to be in use sometime during the eighties, and legislation will undoubtedly follow. Meanwhile, no one at any age should drive or be driven by someone under the influence of marijuana.

Is Marijuana Addictive? Very high, frequent doses of THC can produce a mild physical dependence complete with withdrawal symptoms such as irritability, sleep problems, digestive upsets, and loss of appetite. There is also some evidence of psychological dependence in which users may feel they need the drug regularly in order to cope with life. Daily users are much more likely than moderate users to say they smoke marijuana to escape problems, get through the day, or deal with anger and frustration. It has further been established that users develop a tolerance to THC — that is, that higher doses are eventually needed to achieve the same effects.

Does Marijuana Lead to the Use of Other Drugs? The "steppingstone" theory is tricky. Marijuana regularly precedes the use of other illicit drugs. And alcohol and tobacco often precede the use of marijuana. These relationships are strong, but not inevitable. Many youngsters (about 35 percent of the 1981 high school seniors who had used illicit drugs) use marijuana exclusively. Nor is there any proof that alcohol, tobacco, or marijuana *causes* the use of additional drugs. It may be simply that those who are inclined to try one of the "entry-level" drugs at an early age are also inclined to try other drugs later on. It's also possible that early users become involved with drug-oriented friends who encourage diversity in drug use.

But whether marijuana causes the use of other drugs or is related in some more subtle way is not terribly important to parents. *The fact is that kids who use alcohol, tobacco, or marijuana are much more likely to use other drugs.* The relationship is especially strong among daily pot smokers. In 1980, high school seniors who smoked marijuana on a daily basis used other illicit drugs five to seven times more often than the total twelfth grade population. It's also true that the earlier a child uses alcohol, tobacco, or marijuana, the more likely he or she is to go on to other drugs.

Does Marijuana Cause Burnout or Lack of Motivation? "Burnouts," in drug terminology, are people who are dull, move slowly, have trouble thinking and remembering, and can't stay tuned in to their surroundings. There is evidence that some exceptionally heavy users do not recover full brain function when the drug is discontinued. But marijuana burnout probably more often describes someone who is currently involved in heavy use. Either way, the condition is tragic.

Marijuana also has a reputation for causing apathy, lack of motivation, and unconcern for the future. Although the scientific evidence is mixed, there are many indications that the reputation is based on fact. For one thing, drug care professionals report seeing the symptoms fairly often. For another, marijuana is known to have a sedative effect. Finally, regular users report experiencing the condition. Forty-two percent of daily marijuana users among high school seniors report that the drug causes a loss of energy and almost a third believe it reduces their interest in other activities.

An Area of Agreement. One marijuana issue that is not controversial is the danger of the drug to children. The hazards to health and adolescent development mandate that parents be actively concerned.

Parents have worked effectively in many of the marijuana problem's public aspects — successfully campaigning for laws to control paraphernalia stores, for example. The parent movement's educational effort is partly responsible for the recent drop in marijuana smoking among high school students. Many other anti-drug activities that need the help of parents are described in chapter seven.

The most important role of parents in the marijuana struggle, however, will continue to be on the home front. The size and economic importance of the marijuana industry are indications that the drug will not be stamped out in the early future. For some time to come, marijuana will remain a reality that youngsters must be equipped to cope with. And therein lies the priority for parents: our first order of business must be to strengthen our own children's defenses. They need our help learning to manage themselves in a world that will continue to confront them with both opportunity and pressure to smoke pot.

Chapter Six

The other drugs

Variety has always been a feature of the American marketplace. As a nation, we've been able to choose from dozens of deodorants, automobile models, and flavors of ice cream. Now, in the same tradition, our kids can choose from dozens of dangerous drugs.

There are downers for the uptight, uppers for the downhearted, mind expanders for the adventurous, cocaine for the rich, inhalants for the young, poor, and foolhardy. And, for parents, there is confusion and worry.

Lest there also be despair, remember that the majority of young people do not use the drugs described in this chapter. Among those who were seniors in 1981, 34 percent had never used an illicit drug and another 23 percent had used only marijuana. Not even the kids in that 57 percent, however, can avoid dealing with the issue. Drugs loom so large in the adolescent landscape that all young people have to deal with them somehow. They may decide to abstain, experiment, practice moderation, or go whole hog, but the point is they must decide. When they do, they need (if not always seem wholeheartedly to appreciate) parents who are informed, involved, and supportive.

STIMULANTS

The use of stimulants is growing faster among high school seniors than any other drug, including alcohol or marijuana. The drugs that the kids call speed (amphetamines and their substitutes) are more likely to be used at school than alcohol and marijuana. They are very hard on the body. And, because they are often manufactured illegally in bootleg laboratories (not to mention basements and garages), they are extremely unreliable. There is no way young people can know exactly what they're taking when they swallow street speed.

What They Are. Amphetamine-type drugs speed up body processes (blood pressure, pulse rate, alertness, physical strength, breathing) by stimulating the central nervous system, including the brain. They can be taken orally or injected, although injection is not common among adolescents. Many different amphetamines are available on both the legal and illegal markets. Some of those you may have heard about are Benzedrine, Dexedrine, Methedrine, and Biphetamine. Amphetamine-like drugs include Preludin, Ritalin, Tenuate, and many others. The kids themselves often don't know which amphetamine they're taking. They recognize them as "whites" (small white pills) or "black beauties" (large black capsules), but beyond that, they tend to be as uninformed as we are.

Amphetamines have been around only for about fifty years. Americans were first introduced to the drugs by the Benzedrine inhaler, which made its appearance in drugstores in 1932. Very early on, amphetamines were discovered by college students, truck drivers, and performers. In all three cases, the drugs were (and are) used to stay awake and alert, whether for the purpose of passing exams, driving long hours, or "getting up" for a performance. Millions of Americans also have taken amphetamines as diet pills, and they have been widely used in combat since World War II. Their recreational use dates from the 1960s, when they were discovered by the west coast drug culture.

Who Uses Them. Stimulants (including over-the-counter products) are used by more high school students than any other illicit drug except marijuana. Curiously, they are the one illicit drug used by more girls (57 percent of whom say they use them as a diet aid) than boys. The use of stimulants among high school students grew steadily throughout the seventies, and continued to grow as marijuana use declined at the beginning of the eighties. In 1981, 32 percent of the national senior class had used stimulants at least once and 16 percent had used them during the month before the survey. Roughly two-thirds of the students who use these drugs have mixed them with marijuana and/or alcohol.

While the use of amphetamines among high school students has been increasing, the number of those who report using them to get high has declined. The reason given most often by youngsters for using the drugs is "to get more energy." Large numbers of kids also report using amphetamines to stay awake, and to help lose weight.

Their Effects. Medically speaking, the amphetamines speed up a number of body processes. As is the case with all drugs, the effects reported by users vary. Most commonly, the person is more wakeful, more alert, more energetic and excited, more talkative, more confident, and less hungry. Some of the ill effects that users experience (usually as a result of a large dose or prolonged use) are dry mouth, sleeplessness, headache, hyperactivity, mental confusion, paranoia, hallucinations, and aggressive, violent behavior. The use of amphetamines can also lead to psychological dependence, malnutrition, heart damage, and stroke. Although the death rate is not high, an overdose can cause death from convulsions that lead to respiratory failure.

Heavy users of amphetamines sometimes get into a pattern (called a run) of staying high for several hours or even days at a time, and then crashing. The problem with this practice is that while the body may seem inexhaustible during a high, it isn't. The aftermath of amphetamine intoxication is physical exhaustion and, in some cases, depression. In extreme cases, the straight world may look so bleak upon reentry that the user becomes suicidal.

False Amphetamines. A fairly recent development in the illicit drug field is the sale of counterfeit drugs. Since 1980, look-alike drugs (pills and capsules manufactured to resemble illicit drugs in high demand) have been sweeping the country. They are advertised in magazines and sold in thriving mail-order operations. Look-alike amphetamines, Quaaludes, and cocaine are all in wide distribution. Several states have passed laws against look-alikes, and federal authorities have taken action against their manufacturers and mail-order suppliers.

False amphetamines (the most frequent counterfeit) usually contain caffeine and/or decongestants. Ironically, these pretenders may be more dangerous than the real thing. One of the most troublesome ingredients is a decongestant called phenylpropanolamine or PPA. PPA can cause sudden large increases in blood pressure that can lead to stroke. A number of deaths have been reported from PPA, from another amphetamine-substitute called ephedrine, and even from massive doses of caffeine.

Another danger is that kids taking pseudo-speed may believe they have developed tolerance to high doses of genuine amphetamines and, consequently, may overdose when they happen to get the real thing. All in all, the look-alike drugs are beginning to look like another episode of trouble.

COCAINE

Cocaine is the status stimulant. It has come a long way, from its humble use for centuries by South American mountaineers who pick it from bushes for free, to its present position as a super-expensive drug that hip North Americans put up their noses. The economics of cocaine are as dizzying as the rest of its effects—the ounce of pure cocaine that cost about $35 if bought legally from a drug company in 1980 commonly sold for thousands of dollars on the street when it had been diluted and divided into smaller quantities.

What It Is. Cocaine is a white powder made from the leaves of the South American coca shrub. It stimulates the central nervous system, much like the amphetamines. Some users insist that a cocaine high is more intense and pleasant than one produced by an amphetamine, although others suggest that the drug's status has more to do with its price than its desirability. In this country, cocaine is usually sniffed into the nasal cavity, although it also can be injected or smoked. Natives of the Andes Mountains, where the coca plant grows, chew its leaves to keep themselves going in a thin atmosphere with a small food supply.

Around the turn of the century, cocaine was widely available in this country. It was an ingredient of Coca-Cola, as well as many patent medicines and tonics. During the early 1900s, the drug was forced underground by legislation. It remained there, as a vice of the rich and pampered, until it emerged to join the other drugs on the 1960s street scene.

Who Uses It. The use of cocaine by adolescents rose very sharply during the last half of the 1970s. The number of kids who had used the drug during their senior year in high school more than doubled during the years 1975-79 (from 5.6 to 12 percent). The increase continued, though at a much lower rate, in 1980-81. Much high school cocaine use is experimental or occasional.

Like most drugs, cocaine is used by more boys than girls and by more students not headed for college. In 1980-81, however, the cocaine use of kids who were not college-bound leveled off, while the increase continued among those who planned to go to college. Young people from the western and northeastern parts of the country use far more cocaine than those from other areas.

Its Effects. Cocaine speeds up the same body processes (pulse, temperature, breathing, blood pressure, and others) as the amphetamines. Young people, however, are far less likely to report using cocaine than stimulants to increase energy or stay awake. (The reasons seniors give most often for cocaine use are to feel good or get high, to see what it's like, and to have a good time with friends.)

Users report that cocaine produces a short-lived but seductive feeling of well-being, reduces fatigue, and increases self-confidence, mental ability, and sociability. At high doses, it also can cause restlessness, overexcitability, and confusion during the high period, as well as depression, anxiety, fatigue, and a desire for more cocaine when the effects wear off. Very high doses can lead to convulsions. Regular use can result in serious psychological dependence, a chronic runny nose, sleeplessness, loss of appetite, and even a strange psychosis involving hallucination of bugs crawling on or under the skin. Unless they're also crawling with money, chronic users invariably run into serious financial problems.

A particularly hazardous form of cocaine is known on the street as "free base." This potent variety is obtained by chemically processing the more common form of the drug, often by means of an amateur lab kit sold in paraphernalia stores. Free-base cocaine, which is smoked rather than snorted, is dangerous because of its high potency and rapid absorption into the body through the lungs. "Free basing" is much more likely to produce dependence than snorting, and there can be (depending on the chemicals involved) a risk of explosion while the drug is being processed.

Some of the other problems that occur with cocaine result not from the drug itself but from materials mixed with it. Street cocaine rarely contains more than 10 to 12 percent cocaine. For obvious economic reasons, it is mixed with various sugars, powdered Vitamin B, amphetamines, and a number of local anesthetics.

Look-alike products have also been showing up recently as ingredients of street cocaine. The cocaine look-alikes are sold legally as incense by paraphernalia stores under trade names like "Pseudocaine" and "Toot." They usually contain caffeine, phenylpropanolamine (PPA), and benzocaine (an anesthetic).

The number of deaths from cocaine increased sharply along with its rate of use during the 1970s. Generally speaking, the widespread abuse of cocaine is discouraged by its price. Whenever it is readily available, however, it more than holds its own as a problem drug.

DEPRESSANTS

The depressant drugs are sometimes called "solid alcohol." They produce many of the same effects as alcohol, with varying degrees of danger. All of them work by depressing the central nervous system. Depending upon how much, how often, and how long they're used, the depressants can bring about relaxation, relief from worry, sleep, coma, or death.

Depressants (also called sedative-hypnotics) are subclassified as barbiturates, nonbarbiturate sedatives, and tranquilizers. Barbiturates are among the most dangerous drugs available to adolescents. Nonbarbiturate sedatives include the drug methaqualone (Quaaludes), a harmful drug whose popularity is growing. Tranquilizers are the drugs kids are most likely to find in their parents' medicine chests. All of these drugs are especially dangerous and unpredictable when they're mixed with each other or with alcohol.

Barbiturates. Barbiturates are the drugs that old-style movie stars used to fall afoul of. Some of the familiar brands are Seconal (reds), Nembutal (yellows), Tuinal (rainbows), Amytal, and phenobarbital. Like most drugs in the medical repertoire, barbiturates were considered wonder drugs when they were introduced in 1903. For more than fifty years, they were widely prescribed for relief of anxiety, nervousness, insomnia, and seizures. Unfortunately, these drugs turned out to have some very dangerous effects. Since their widespread abuse in the 1960s and the introduction of less dangerous drugs with some of the same functions, doctors have prescribed them much less frequently.

Heavy use of barbiturates quickly produces tolerance and a dependence from which withdrawal is dangerous. Barbiturate withdrawal, which should be attempted only under medical supervision, may include delirium, vomiting, high body temperatures, shakiness, and convulsions that can lead to death.

Another danger of these drugs is their narrow safety margin. That is, after tolerance has developed, the large doses needed to produce the desired effect are closer to the lethal level. The unknown strength of street barbiturates and the tendency of heavy users to forget how much they've taken then add to the danger of fatal overdose. Along with heroin and other narcotics, the barbiturates are among the leading causes of drug deaths across the country.

The number of adolescents who use barbiturates is decreasing. Less fortunately, almost 60 percent of the seniors who have used these drugs have tried the potentially fatal combination of barbiturates and alcohol.

Quaaludes and Other Nonbarbiturates. Methaqualone is one of the drugs on the increase among high school students, who know it as Sopors, Quaaludes, ludes, and 714s (among other names). This alcohol-like drug began a second climb in the statistics (it had been popular earlier in the decade) near the end of the 1970s. Nationally in 1981, methaqualone had been used at some time by 10.6 percent of all seniors. In my community, the figure was 13-15 percent.

Like alcohol, Quaaludes often produce a noisy, uncoordinated, aggressive drunk, likely to have a hangover in the morning. Quaalude intoxication is proving to be a menace on the highway. The drug is particularly dangerous and even lethal in combination with alcohol or other depressants. It can produce physical dependence with a set of potentially fatal withdrawal symptoms. Finally, because so much of it is manufactured by amateur chemists, neither the content nor the potency of street methaqualone can be trusted. Look-alike methaqualone is common.

Other nonbarbiturate sedatives, which have many of the same properties as methaqualone but are not as widely used by young people, include Doriden, Placidyl, Noludar and others.

Tranquilizers. Tranquilizers rank high among the drugs kids are likely to catch their parents popping. Among high school students, Valium is still the clear favorite. Librium is a poor second and the others are far behind.

Nationally, in 1981, these drugs had been used at least once by 14.7 percent of all high school seniors. Boys use slightly more tranquilizers than girls (the reverse is true among adults). More kids say they use tranquilizers for their relaxing qualities than for the high, although the high is also rated important.

Tranquilizers are used and overused medically for the treatment of anxiety, tension, insomnia, and tense muscles. Those classified as benzodiazepines (Valium, Librium, Ativan, Serax, Tranxene) have a wider safety margin than the barbiturates. That is, death from overdose is unusual, although not unheard of. When very large doses are taken, or when heavy doses are taken over a long period of time, these "minor tranquilizers" can have all the disadvantages of the other depressants. Most tranquilizers can produce tolerance and lead to both psychological and physical dependence, in some cases with severe withdrawal symptoms.

Another group of drugs (Equanil, Miltown and others) are classified as tranquilizers but have more dangerous, barbiturate-like effects. All tranquilizers are more potent in combination with alcohol or other depressants.

HALLUCINOGENS

Alice's ticket to Wonderland may have been a hallucinogen. Her growing and shrinking and some of her other sensations suggest she may have been eating more than marmalade. The hallucinogenic trips taken by present-day Alices and Als apparently can be just as strange and full of wonder — or frightening and dangerous, depending on which part of the rabbit hole they land in.

To hallucinate means to see, hear, or experience real surroundings in an unusual way, or to have visions — to see, hear, or otherwise sense events and surroundings that are not material. Hallucinogens are also called psychedelics, a word that comes from a Greek term meaning "to show the soul." Hallucinogenic drugs have been used throughout history in religious rites and are believed by some contemporary users to provide spiritual or personal insight. Their more common use today, however, is as party drugs. Far more high school seniors, for example, report using LSD to have a good time with their friends than to seek deeper insight.

The effects of hallucinogens vary greatly from drug to drug, from setting to setting, from episode to episode, and from person to person. Users say it's all but impossible to describe a hallucinogenic experience, although some have tried. If you're interested in an account, I'd recommend the one, written by a journalist who took LSD unawares, in Tom Wolfe's *The Electric Kool-Aid Acid Test*.

LSD. Unbeknownst to most parents of the 1960s, the Beatles had more in mind than a heavenly young lady when they sang "Lucy in the Sky with Diamonds." Kids in the know listened for the initials. The influence of LSD was everywhere in the 60s youth culture — from its music to its lighting effects to its emphasis on soul-searching. The wavy, reverse-image television pictures that are popular today are a manifestation that had to wait for technology to catch up.

Even among the postadolescent drug culture, the use of LSD declined during the 70s. Among adolescents, its use has always been largely experimental, although there are some youthful "acid heads."

D-lysergic acid diethylamide (LSD) is a synthetic hallucinogen. It is extremely potent, so that a teaspoonful can yield thousands of doses. The drug is taken as a pill, a capsule, a small paper square (blotter), or gelatin chip (windowpane). Like other hallucinogens, LSD has varying effects. The drug can produce vivid colors, lighting effects, and shifting forms — a sort of sensory multi-media event.

LSD can also produce unpleasant hallucinations (the so-called bad trip), panic reactions, psychoses, and flashbacks. Since all LSD available today is manufactured illegally, its purity and potency are always in question. Negative effects are most likely to occur among the psychologically unstable, another condition that is hard to gauge in the nonscientific settings where virtually all LSD is taken. (The setting is important — users are most likely to report positive experiences if they take LSD in a relaxed, pleasant atmosphere among people they trust.) The effects can be terrifying to the point of mental illness when people are given LSD unknowingly. In 1980, a fourth of the high school students who had taken the drug reported at least one bad trip.

PCP. Phencyclidine (PCP or angel dust) has a bad reputation even among drug users. Its last legal use was as an anesthetic for large animals — a fact that should suggest some of its drawbacks as a recreational drug for humans. The drug had a brief heyday during the sixties when it was taken in pill form. Then, for a number of years, it was out of favor. A new PCP epidemic began in the early 1970s when young people discovered the drug was easier to control if it was smoked or snorted. Its principal attraction apparently is "more bang for the buck" — it produces a fast, intense high at a comparatively low cost.

Around 1980, PCP use began to decline sharply again. The twin tragedies that remain are the drug's high degree of danger and its popularity among young teenagers. Medics in Seattle, for example, report that most of those who O.D. at rock concerts are fourteen or younger. These children are most likely to use PCP and least likely to have the necessary resources to use it without courting disaster.

PCP comes in a variety of forms, including pills, powder, liquid, crystal, and combinations with parsley and other leafy materials. Its classification as a hallucinogen is disputed. Across the country, it goes by more than forty names including angel dust, tick, crystal, buzz, monkey dust, rocket fuel, and others. PCP has consistently been misrepresented as THC — the active ingredient in marijuana. As late as 1979, more high school students believed they had used THC, which was not yet available, than PCP. (Now that THC is being produced for therapeutic use by hospitals, it can be expected to show up increasingly often on the street.)

The effects of PCP are unpredictable, except that so many of them are bad. A heavy dose of the drug (which is after all an anesthetic) may immobilize the user, making it difficult to move, talk, think, or remember. Burnout is common among chronic users. Those who become over-agitated often injure themselves because they are literally "feeling no pain." A number of disoriented users have drowned when they have been unable to find the top of the swimming pool or bathtub. The drug also can lead to violence, psychosis, and severe psychological depression as well as a number of medical problems that are potentially fatal.

Other Hallucinogens. In 1980, more high school seniors believed they had tried mescaline, the psychoactive ingredient of the peyote cactus, than any other hallucinogen except LSD. In reality, many of the drugs sold as mescaline *are* LSD or another substitute. A few students have eaten peyote itself, which has been used in religious ceremonies for centuries by various Indian tribes. The effects of mescaline and peyote are similar to those of LSD.

A few high school students have tried psilocybin, the active ingredient in hallucinogenic mushrooms. Supermarket mushrooms are sometimes sprayed with PCP or LSD and sold as psilocybins. One of the dangers of "doing mushrooms" is the possibility of eating a poisonous variety.

In the Cincinnati area, the hallucinogen that hospitalizes more adolescents than all other drugs of abuse put together is Jimson weed, a drug substance not covered by the high school survey! Other hallucinogens not included on the survey are the seeds of some varieties of morning glory, and a number of amphetamine/psychedelics with names like government agencies: DOM (also known as STP), MDA, MDM, DMT, DOB, PMA, and TMA.

INHALANTS

The list of things kids are sniffing for kicks is literally open-ended. By this time tomorrow, some youngster will have discovered another one, probably from a container marked "contents harmful if inhaled." The inhalants, which are big favorites of young adolescents, fall roughly into four categories: solvents, aerosol products, nitrous oxide, and the amyl and butyl nitrites.

A few of the many solvents that are sniffed (or "huffed" as the practice is known by a lot of kids) are gasoline, glue, model airplane cement, dry cleaning fluid, transmission and brake fluid, fingernail polish remover, liquid shoe polish, wax strippers, degreasers, paint, lacquer, and lacquer thinner. Garages, basements, and the cupboard under the sink offer endless possibilities.

The nonstick cooking sprays were among the first aerosols discovered by sniffers. Eventually, everything from hairspray to insecticide has been inhaled. Bronze, gold, and clear lacquers have been used heavily in some areas.

Amyl nitrite was originally used medically for the treatment of angina. It comes in small crushable glass bulbs that users call "poppers" or "snappers." Unlike other inhalants, this one traveled down to adolescents from older drug users who believe it lengthens and heightens orgasm. Once the demand had been established, underground enterprise quickly moved to supply an over-the-counter version, butyl nitrite, sold under trade names like Locker Room, Rush, Kick, Bullet, and Jac Aroma. Some of these products are thinly disguised as room odorizers that dispense the aroma (for which demand must be fairly narrow) of a sweaty locker room. Another inhalant used illicitly is the anesthetic, nitrous oxide or laughing gas.

The Effects of Sniffing. The short-term effects of inhalants are similar to those of alcohol: giddiness, loss of inhibition, mental confusion, clumsiness, and blackout. Many inhalants can produce death by suffocation. High concentrations of aerosol sprays can produce instant death from heart failure—a result common enough to have been given the medical nickname, "sudden sniffing death." Aerosols also involve a host of dangers from their non-intoxicating contents. In the process of inhaling the intoxicant, youngsters also may get insecticide, disinfectant, or whatever else is in the can.

Long-term effects are harder to pin down because of a lack of tracking and because chronic sniffers are likely to muddy the waters by combining drugs. The information collected from workers exposed to industrial solvents, however, indicates that long-term sniffers can experience damage to the nervous system, liver, kidneys, blood, and bone marrow.

Who Uses Inhalants. Inhalants are sometimes used by children as young as seven or eight, even before they have tried alcohol or tobacco. The common age to begin is around twelve or thirteen. In the twelve to seventeen age-group, more kids (about nine to ten percent) have used inhalants than any other illicit drug except marijuana. This is a statistical distortion caused by the large number of very young teenagers who are sniffers. Older teenagers tend to regard inhalants as low-status kid-stuff drugs, although some continue to use them.

One of the reasons that very young children use inhalants is that they're easy to come by. You don't need connections to get a can of varnish. Inhalants are also less expensive and easier to explain than alcohol or marijuana. Shoe polish doesn't usually bring on a lot of questions from grownups. Because of the cost factor, sniffing is common in low-income neighborhoods. It is usually a group activity, and peer influence is all-important. Kids tend to use the particular inhalant considered cool by the peer group, which also decides how, when, where, and how much inhalant abuse takes place. Finally, a lot of youngsters give the usual reasons: "it feels good" or "I like the high."

NARCOTICS

Narcotics are the "old" drugs that we used to associate with desperate urban junkies. Medically, these drugs are used as sedatives and pain relievers and for the relief of diarrhea and coughing. The natural narcotics, or opiates, are products of the opium poppy: opium, morphine, and codeine. Heroin is a derivative of morphine. There also are a number of synthetic narcotics such as methadone, Demerol, Darvon, Dilaudid, Talwin, and others.

The narcotics are not widely used among adolescents. Only 1.1 percent of 1981 high school seniors admitted to ever having used heroin. A much larger group (10.1 percent) had used other narcotics including, in order of popularity, codeine, opium, Demerol, methadone, morphine, and others. Codeine (often taken in cough syrup) is a big favorite, even among kids who have barely experimented with hard drugs.

The principal long-term problem associated with narcotics is dependence. Heroin involves a difficult, lengthy, and well-publicized withdrawal. Contrary to popular belief, however, heroin withdrawal is not as dangerous as that of alcohol or barbiturates. Another heroin myth, disproved by the Vietnam experience, is that the drug is permanently addictive. More than 70 percent of the servicemen who used heroin in Vietnam stopped when they came home.

Narcotic addicts often suffer from malnutrition, brought on by lack of funds or disinterest in eating. Those who inject the drugs are also prone to infections and hepatitis, spread by unsanitary hypodermic equipment.

Narcotic overdose causes depression of the central

nervous system with slow pulse and breathing, possible unconsciousness, and fairly frequent death. Nationally, among all age-groups, narcotics are involved in more emergency-room deaths than any other drug family. Heroin and methadone are the principal offenders, either on their own or in combination with alcohol and barbiturates. Codeine, the teenage favorite, also occasionally causes death.

Opium, which has been around for most of human history, is second only to codeine as the narcotic of choice among adolescents. For centuries, this natural drug was used not only for pleasure but as one of the few available remedies for pain. In the 1800s, the British fought two wars with China to protect their profitable "Indian connection." The nineteenth century also saw the development of morphine, codeine, and the hypodermic needle. Injected morphine, which was extremely important as a pain reliever during the Civil War, led to the addiction of large numbers of soldiers. During the second half of the century, the Chinese introduced opium smoking to this country, and traveling medicine men and drug stores sold patent medicine liberally laced with narcotics. American opiate addiction was at its all-time high around 1900.

Heroin was introduced in the 1890s. Like most new drugs, it was considered a godsend—a non-habit-forming substitute for other opiates! This notion had been disproved long before the heroin epidemic of the 1950s and 60s developed in American inner cities. Currently, although not a large problem on a national basis, heroin use remains high among young males in urban areas. That doesn't mean, of course, that it never happens elsewhere: students in a suburb with relatively low overall drug use told me that "a couple of kids out here" use heroin. On the whole, however, high school narcotics users are much more likely to take cough medicine or age-old opium.

SOME AFTERTHOUGHTS

Like me, you may be shocked at the variety of drugs available to our children. You may feel, as I do, that you've just completed a tour of a minefield where young people can't avoid spending time. It's important to remember, at a time like this, that most kids get through the adolescent years intact. A large number experiment with drugs and then forget it. Even among those who use drugs regularly, not everyone has a life-threatening experience or ends up addicted.

Most kids won't have serious drug problems. But all kids are in some degree of danger, if only by proximity. That's why we're all in this together. Every parent has a stake in deterring drug abuse, first in the home, then in the community and nation.

Chapter Seven

Prevention: what you can do

The drug problem is like a bundle of snarled string — all loose ends, knots, and tangles. It has legal, financial, legislative, educational, medical, judicial, personal, psychological, and social aspects — all of which are knotty. Consequently, no single person, group, or institution can solve the problem. Nor can ten thousand people pulling on a single string. Undoing the drug dilemma will require the combined efforts of the whole national community — a lot of people methodically untangling a lot of strings.

A number of programs for dealing with drug problems are described on the pages that follow. These methods have been gathered both from research and from my conversations (whether face-to-face or written) with students, parents, and drug and family counselors around the country. I hope you'll apply many of the family prevention measures explained here, then (if time and energy permit) pick one or two activities from the many described for schools and communities. But don't take on so many projects that you find yourself neglecting the one that's most important. Drug prevention is an enterprise in which our kids come first.

Try to think of this chapter as a catalog, rather than an operational handbook. Space doesn't permit step-by-step instructions for setting up the programs. In each case, however, I've included at least one resource you can use to get more information. Addresses for all of the organizations mentioned are listed at the end of chapter eight.

FAMILY PREVENTION

Dr. Stephen Glenn, a nationally known teacher of parenting, likes to say that children come into the world with empty toolboxes. The human baby is one of the earth's most dependent creatures. In babies, the quality is endearing. Adolescents who remain highly dependent, however, are prone to drug abuse and other problems. Family drug prevention therefore must stress helping kids develop skills (judgment, self-discipline, responsibility, and others) to manage their own lives constructively.

The concept of tools kids can use for themselves is important. Earlier and earlier with each generation, young people have to deal with the world independently. Therefore, the training we give even the youngest children must look to the future. It isn't enough to make our kids eat broccoli when we say to. Later on, they'll need to be able to *choose* a healthful diet *for themselves* from a menu loaded with junk food.

They'll also have to deal, largely on their own, with pressure to use alcohol and drugs. Fortunately, the skills kids need to deal with these and other problems can be provided for in the home — the earlier the better.

But filling children's toolboxes is a tougher job for us than it was for our grandparents. For one thing, adolescence has become riskier and more complicated. For another, because of the changes described in an earlier chapter, some of the tooling up that used to occur almost automatically now requires special attention. A sense of being needed, for example, was hard to avoid in frontier America. If a child forgot to milk the cow, the whole family went without milk, cottage cheese, and butter (and the cow suffered, too). Our kids don't have as many natural opportunities to learn responsibility.

The catalog of tools that follows isn't intended as a

manual for raising children. It offers principles rather than prescriptions. If you have trouble translating these principles into day-to-day family life, you may find help in a parenting course or support group. Those who would like to locate or establish courses may use the addresses of the parent-training organizations listed at the end of chapter eight. You'll probably also find that your library has recent books on parenting and families. My favorites are listed in this book's bibliography.

A note of caution: don't berate yourself for occasionally slipping off the path you've set out to follow in parenting. Any kid will tell you there's no such thing as a perfect parent. The important thing is to keep heading in the right direction, rather than never to take a misguided step.

Here then are some of the tools identified by Dr. Glenn (and interpreted by me) that kids need not only to avoid drug use, but to deal with the world successfully. Dr. Glenn discusses these skills as well as some specific ways parents can help children attain them in his book, *Strengthening the Family*, described in the bibliography.

• *Children need to be able to exercise self-discipline, self-assessment, and self-control.* These skills are essential if a child is to resist following the crowd into drug use. Parents can nurture the skills of self-conduct by giving kids *guided* opportunities for practice. Self-discipline, for example, involves putting aside what we want to do at the moment in order to achieve something of value. Parents can teach the skill neither by punishing nor indulging a child's misguided act, but by allowing its natural consequences to happen. The child who comes home late for dinner thus will be met with "I'm sorry you missed your dinner — better luck next time," rather than "I'm taking away your allowance" or "Your dinner is in the oven." Parents need to take active roles as guides and coaches, helping kids understand what goes wrong (or right) as they practice independence. One technique for guiding children is the teaching question ("What could you do to remind yourself to get home in time for dinner?").

● *Children need the ability to operate successfully within a system.* The systems involved may be formal (school) or informal (a sandlot softball game). The tool that is needed is responsibility, based on an understanding of cause-and-effect, limits, and consequences. Kids must be able to recognize those factors in a situation ("It may be okay to skip my homework tonight, but if I do it very often, I'll lose my eligibility for soccer"). They must learn to adapt their behavior ("I'll do the homework") in order to get their needs met ("because I live for soccer"). Kids who can't fulfill their needs within a system are prone to drug abuse and other problem dependencies. They're also likely to blame others for the grief they come to ("I wouldn't be using drugs if Mrs. McMeany hadn't flunked me in math and washed me out of soccer").

Again, parents can help by providing guidance and by letting children experience consequences within the family system. It should be noted that teaching the lesson of consequences can be difficult for parents whose natural instinct is protection. For young children, the lesson may mean going without lunch if they forget their lunch money repeatedly. For troubled teenagers, it may mean losing driving privileges if they've mixed drinking with driving. It's important that children understand such consequences not as punishment, but as the natural results of their own behavior.

● *Children need positive role models.* They need to believe they can be like other people they see functioning capably. Children also need to be seen by others as capable. Parents can help a great deal by letting kids know their parents believe they're competent.

Role models are also essential to help children acquire values. Children will pick up values from somewhere — if not from parents, then probably from the peer group. Parents need both to express and demonstrate the principles they've chosen to live by. Look for opportunities to explore with your children how your actions are related to your values. If you want honest children, teach and practice honesty. If you want drug-free children, relate drug use to the values you teach and model. Be especially careful what your actions say about your attitude toward healthful living and drug use, including alcohol, tobacco, and tranquilizers.

Religious commitment is often a strong deterrent to drug use. Religion can provide a value system, role models, a source of support and guidance, and often a drug-free peer group.

● *Children need confidence that they can affect what happens to them.* Youngsters who see themselves as victims may turn to alcohol or drugs to escape problems they don't think they can handle. The confidence kids need depends on skill in making judgments, choices, decisions, and game plans *within limits they recognize and understand.*In the early years, the limits children experience are those set and defined by their parents. Kids who don't learn to operate within limits don't learn how their own acts affect them. They bang their heads against the same walls over and over without discovering what's causing the pain.

● *Children need skills for working effectively with others.* Like their parents, they must learn to send and receive communication effectively. They also need the ability to cooperate, give and send feedback, negotiate, share feelings, and empathize. Kids who lack these skills are likely to be frustrated by their inability to interact with others. Parents can help by working hard to improve their own interpersonal skills and by encouraging family interaction.

● *Children need a sense of "family" to which they make contributions and for which they have responsibility.* ("Family," as Dr. Glenn uses the term, can refer not only to the nuclear family, but to other agencies greater than the person. Groups, mankind, God, and country are examples.)

Family activities, traditions, rituals, meals, gatherings, projects, outings, and responsibilities are important. Kids with a sense of family are less likely to use drugs because of a desperate need to belong to a peer group. The experience of sharing goals, efforts, and outcomes has given them a team spirit. They understand that their actions affect the greater family whole that they're a part of.

● *Children need the ability to make judgments.* Making judgments (decisions about what is right, wrong, safe, fair, wise, valuable, and so on) is partly a matter of understanding and applying relationships. Cause-and-effect relationships are important ("My grades are dropping because I can't keep my mind on schoolwork when I've been smoking pot"). Kids also need to be able to go from the general to the specific ("Drinking and driving are a dangerous combination; to me, at this moment, that means I won't get into a car with my friend who has been drinking").

Children learn judgmental skills by being involved with mature people who make judgments and who create opportunities for kids to think through what they would do in the same situation. That is, kids learn by example combined with dialogue. Parents who've established credibility can help kids think through matters related to drug use. What would they do, for example, if they were invited to use drugs at a party?

Parents can also help by permitting kids to follow through on their judgments whenever doing so won't hurt them. We can't allow them to act on a judgment that drugs are okay, for example. But we can let them follow up on a judgment by joining the young Republicans, though we be dyed-in-the-hide Democrats.

All of the skills identified by Dr. Glenn not only discourage drug use, but enhance kids' overall abilities to lead constructive lives. Other observers have pointed out some additional steps parents can take to serve the same dual purpose. Although the principles that follow fit into the Glenn program in some way, they merit special attention:

PREVENTION: WHAT YOU CAN DO

● *Children need to feel they are loved and valued.* This fact turns up in study after study of drug use and other adolescent problems. Most of us love our children, but the message sometimes gets garbled in transmission. What our kids think they're receiving is far more important than what we think we're sending. We should, of course, not hover over or smother our children. Nor should we think that love means approving all their actions. But we need to be sure our kids are aware of our love and support.

● *Children need clearly defined limits.* They need to know what sort of behavior is expected of them, and what they can be sure will happen if they act otherwise. Limits give kids a sense of having dependable surroundings. They also form a framework in which children acquire confidence and responsibility by learning how their acts, choices, and decisions affect what happens to them.

Rules should be reasonable and designed to protect kids. They should have teaching value and be administered with firmness, dignity, and love for the offender. Limits enforced with hostility or chronic inconsistency can be as damaging as lack of limits.

As kids grow older, it's vitally important that they learn to set their own limits. For parents, this is a matter of carefully lengthening the tether. Whenever possible, we need to give our children opportunities to practice self-discipline. As they do, our job is to coach, serve as good examples, and cheerlead.

● *Children need to develop self-esteem.* One of the characteristics of drug-free families is that they don't put down their children. They're able to separate what their children *do* from what they *are*. The child as a person receives unqualified love and support, even when his or her actions call for disapproval.

All of the skills of capability identified by Dr. Glenn (discussed earlier in this chapter) promote healthy self-concepts. Parents can also encourage self-esteem by making sure kids have opportunities for service, accomplishment, and recognition. We need to encourage our children to pursue their interests, while we lead the cheers. Most of us need to spend less time pointing out our children's errors, and much more time applauding their successes. Kids who feel appreciated, worthwhile, and successful have special protection.

● *Children need open, honest communication with their parents.* This is the need mentioned most often by the drug care professionals I heard from. Kids need to be able to express their feelings, joys, and problems without fear. One counselor pointed out that parents sometimes send a double message of "I want you to share everything with me" and "If you ever tell me you're doing such and such, I'll kill you." Parents who want to communicate honestly with their children need to be somewhat shockproof.

Parents also need to express their own feelings honestly. Don't insist nothing is wrong as you bang the silverware. Your kids won't believe you, and they'll be sure to pick up on your example when *they* are upset. What's worse, they may sense you don't think them important enough to warrant honesty.

Finally, parents need to listen effectively. The complaint registered most often by teenagers is "adults don't listen to us." Dr. Glenn and others stress the importance of "active listening," which involves imagining, analyzing, and interacting with the other person's experience.

For most of us, good listening requires training. Most parenting courses include communication practice, and courses devoted exclusively to communication are popping up everywhere on the schedules of community service organizations (YMCA's, Family Service, public adult schools, and so on). For do-it-yourselfers, I've listed a helpful book in the bibliography.

Some Specific Anti-Drug Measures. Over and over, drug counselors emphasize that parents need to educate themselves about drugs and drug use. No one can deal with any problem from a position of ignorance. Don't stop with this book. You'll need to find out what's going on in your own community, your schools, and your children's friendship circles.

Once you've become informed, talk about the drug situation calmly with your children. Tell them about your feelings, your worries, and your stand on drug use. Be ready to listen and discuss (not fight about) their feelings and concerns. Make sure your children have accurate drug information, and that they clearly understand the family limits on drug use. Let them know they can count on you to help in this, as in all situations, although you cannot promise to rescue them from the consequences of drug use. For suggestions on how to handle drug use — whether experimental, regular, or dependent — see chapter eight.

A parent group (Community Action Against Drug Abuse) in Sacramento, California, has drawn up and distributed a set of guidelines for parents to follow. Those who take the "Parent's Pledge" agree to

- develop and communicate a clear position about drug and alcohol use.
- not serve drugs or alcohol to others' children.
- support school and law enforcement policy regarding use of drugs and alcohol and encourage the use of creative and effective discipline in dealing with offenders.
- request and endorse a comprehensive drug and alcohol abuse prevention program for grades kindergarten through twelve.
- be concerned about the welfare of others, resist peer pressure, and encourage youth to do likewise.
- promote wholesome social activities for youth and not sponsor or condone social activities parents or children cannot control.
- become informed parents who take responsibility for their children.
- set an example that can be copied by children and try not to confuse them with double standards.
- remember that appropriate and consistent discipline

conveys concern and love to children.

I would like to propose two simple amendments to the CADA guidelines. First, while I agree parents should take responsibility for their children, I think they should not do so excessively — that is, to the point that children are deprived of the opportunity to learn *self*-responsibility. In the same vein, I would add the reminder that "appropriate discipline" will be administered with respect, affection, and concern for the development of self-discipline in the child.

Another measure that has been helpful both in preventing and dealing with drug use in many communities is a network among the parents of a group of children who are friends. These groups not only provide support for parents, but they make life easier for children, who find it easier to resist drugs when they're taboo for the entire peer group. Parents in a network can be confident their children are in good hands at their friends' homes and that parties are chaperoned. For help in setting up such a group, refer to Marsha Manatt's book, *Parents Peers and Pot* (described in the bibliography), or send for a copy of the *Parent Group Starter Kit*, available for $2 from the National Federation of Parents for Drug-Free Youth.

SCHOOL PROGRAMS

Schools are much less likely to take the ostrich approach to drug problems nowadays. A school drug program often begins when a principal or group of teachers gets tired of kids passing out in the parking lot after games or dances. I found some school officials reluctant to talk about drug problems in their schools with an outsider, but none denied having them. Many would welcome some positive, nonthreatening help from parents.

A growing number of schools have programs for drug prevention (stopping use before it begins) or intervention (stepping in early to help students headed for trouble). If your school district has begun such a program, all you may need to do is find out how to help. The program may need to be interpreted and supported among parents. There undoubtedly will be a need for funds in this day of budget cuts — you might raise money to send a counselor to a training workshop. One school prevention program that I know of (and describe below) is actually conducted by parents.

If your school does not have a prevention or intervention program, your work will require more finesse. A successful school drug program requires the support of the administration, board of education, counseling staff, and teachers. Their time and funds are already overextended, and their first reaction may be to resist *any* new program, no matter what its content. On the other hand, many school officials and teachers are aware that drug problems interfere with education and that there is a strong movement toward dealing with those problems in school systems.

Many school districts begin with a task force or committee, made up of representatives of the school board, administration, faculty, parents, drug prevention and law enforcement agencies. You might start by going to the Superintendent of Schools, privately and tactfully, and offering to serve on or gather resources for such a committee. You also could approach members of the board of education, who are your elected officials. You could support candidates for the school board who are committed to a drug program. You could talk with the officers of your parent-teacher organization. Several state PTA's have been active in the anti-drug movement and National PTA offers an alcohol education program.

What I think you should *not* do is issue a public ultimatum demanding that school officials do something about "their" drug problem. The success of your efforts is likely to hinge on being interpreted as help, not interference.

Your case will be stronger if you can offer some resources as you ask for action. You might prepare by attending workshops, writing to state boards of education and prevention agencies, and talking with people in other school districts. Here are a few programs you and your school may want to look into as you begin:

School Prevention Programs. All around the country, the drug information programs of the 1970s are being replaced with a more active kind of education called prevention. The goal of a prevention program is exactly what its name suggests—to convince children not to begin using drugs. The effort often begins in kindergarten and concentrates on elementary levels. With younger children, information may be directed more to fitness, respect for the mind and body, and careful use of medicine than to the pitfalls of illicit drug use. A prevention program is also likely to include activities to help children strengthen their self-concepts, decision-making skills, and other personal strengths that make it easier to resist peer pressure. Another technique concentrates on books, games, sports, camping, and other ways of turning on without drugs. Most communities now have drug prevention agencies (or prevention specialists within treatment agencies) to help schools plan and carry out prevention programs. The activities may be led by the prevention specialists, teachers, students, or volunteer parents.

Parent Prevention Program. Parents deliver the prevention message in a program developed by Project Pegasus Inc. at Palo Alto, California, with the help of the neighboring Center for Human Development in Lafayette. This program is promising not only because it involves parents, but because it extends the prevention effort at a time of tightening budgets. Either singly or in teams, specially trained parents go into classrooms (kindergarten through grade eight) to lead a university-developed prevention curriculum. The parents receive training before they begin their leadership and periodically through the school year. For information, you may write to Project Pegasus or the Center for Human Development.

Peer Prevention Programs. Prevention programs delivered by teenagers make a lot of sense (provided they're administered by skilled professionals) because of the influence that kids have on each other. Peer pressure, a potent factor in spreading drug use, is harnessed to prevent it. Peer programs also have a number of other advantages. For one thing, they provide an outlet for kids who don't use drugs to go on record and support each other. The young people who take part in the programs also learn skills and attitudes for helping others that will go with them into adult life. They are exposed to caring counselors and other adults who are excellent role models. Peer prevention often benefits both those who give and those who receive the programs.

The Teen Involvement project is one of the older models in the peer prevention field. It trains high school students to serve as advisers, role models, and friends to younger children. The older students present drug information programs in assigned sixth or seventh grade classrooms (just at the age of the first big initiation into drug use). They also offer themselves as older friends the children can call up or come to if they have a problem or need information. The teen advisers don't pose as experts, but are provided with a list of adults they can go to for help or information to pass on to their counselees. The kids I watched training for Teen Involvement had pledged not to use drugs or alcohol during the time they were enrolled in the program. They were warm, outgoing young people that sixth graders would naturally look up to. The National Institute on Drug Abuse has published a manual for students, *Teen Involvement for Drug Abuse Prevention*, and an administrator's guide for the program. Both are available (one copy free) from the National Clearinghouse for Drug Abuse Information.

In other peer prevention programs, students who have received training may staff student information centers, serve as classroom discussion leaders, offer individual counseling, or design their own prevention projects. Some books that offer guidance in setting up and conducting these programs are described in the bibliography.

School Intervention Programs. Intervention programs identify and arrange help for a variety of problems that interfere with education. Intervention requires the support and training of the school's entire professional staff. Teachers are trained to recognize symptoms of problems (which may or may not turn out to be drug-related) and pass the information along discreetly to the counseling staff. A counselor then calls in the student to see if the counseling staff can be helpful. If necessary, the student's parents are also called in for a conference. When students are caught in offenses (using drugs at school, for example) that once would have resulted in suspension or other punishment, they and their families are given the option of treatment. Thus, instead of dumping problems into the street, where they thrive and multiply, intervention programs encourage their solution. Schools that practice intervention often set up support groups for both parents and students. The book, *Harmfully Involved*, by Frank Manning and Jean Vinton, describes the beginnings, structure, and results of one of the country's first intervention programs.

PARENTS IN THE COMMUNITY

Because drug problems have gotten into so many corners, sweeping them out will require a lot of different brooms. Not only parents and educators, but doctors, lawyers, judges, policemen, elected officials, drug care and mental health professionals, clergymen, and merchants need to be involved in a cooperative effort. The instrument that many parents have used to influence, initiate, or plug into such a network is the local parent group.

Although there are variations and some overlap, parent groups fall into two general categories: those organized among parents whose children form a friendship circle (the parent peer group) and those organized to serve a neighborhood, school district, or other slice of the community (the community parent group). Parent peer groups have been described earlier as excellent vehicles to help parents deal with drug problems that directly touch the family. Community parent groups are usually more formally organized and more oriented toward community issues.

The National Federation of Parents for Drug-Free Youth (NFP) provides a *Parent Group Starter Kit* at a cost of $2. The kit gives directions for forming either kind of parent organization. It also describes a host of additional resources for community action, including NFP's own information kits on legislative, law enforcement, drug paraphernalia, publicity, treatment services, and other issues.

Another extremely detailed handbook for organizing an activist parent group is *How to Form a Families in Action Group in Your Community*, by Sue Rusche. This manual contains suggestions for fighting drug paraphernalia stores, as well as for working with law enforcement agencies, the medical community, other community organizations, schools, the entertainment media, and the judicial system.

A different kind of community outreach is provided by a group called Parents In Crisis Inc. in the Buffalo, New York area. This all-volunteer organization offers a number of free services to families whose kids are in trouble. With the help of community professionals, Parents in Crisis stretches a tiny budget to include self-help support groups for parents, referral services, a twenty-four-hour hot line, legal aid, crisis intervention training, and a number of information and prevention programs. This program represents another extension of service in the face of agency budget cuts. It also gives people who have "been there" an opportunity to help others, and its trainees serve as carriers of awareness to the community. If you would like to start a Parents in Crisis chapter in your area, you may write for its *Operational Manual.* Enclose $5 to cover cost of materials and postage.

COOKING POTS AND TOOLKITS

There are obviously more jobs in drug prevention than there are people to fill them. No matter what your interests or abilities, there's a place for you. It's possible, in fact, to make a career of discouraging drug use. Many of the leaders of the national parent movement began as "ordinary" parents concerned about drug use in their own children and communities.

If you're one of those people who can cook on several burners simultaneously, you'll find a lot of pots that need stirring in the drug field. *But remember the priority is your children.* I recommend concentrating first on your own family defenses. Next, I'd work on an interfamily network (a parent peer group). After that, I'd go as far and as wide in the drug fight as my time and energy would take me without neglecting the challenge on the home front.

Eventually, the drug problem will be solved by a coalition of groups and forces, including (perhaps even led by) parents. During the time that matters for our own kids, however, it's a good bet drugs will be around to menace children. And our most important role as parents will continue to be filling toolkits. The best protection we can provide our children will remain a strong, supportive homelife.

Chapter Eight

Dealing with the drug use of your child

Your child is using drugs. You'd like to pretend it isn't happening, but you know it is. The unthinkable must be not only thought about, but dealt with. You feel betrayed, ashamed, and angry.

The first thing you'll need to deal with is your feelings. It isn't that you aren't entitled to some conflicting emotions. It's just that you can't afford to let them complicate the crisis your family is facing. You're going to need a steady heart and hand.

Remember that our kids are living in a different world from the one that existed when many of us were young. Drugs are part of the landscape they've grown up in. The pressures they face to use drugs are strong. Then, too, they've reached the time of life (I'm sure you remember) when kids try things their parents, whose values after all were molded in "the old days," don't approve. Their need for approval is shifting quite naturally, if a bit prematurely, from their parents to their peers.

Remember also that drug use is no longer a symptom of a faulty upbringing. It happens in the wisest and most virtuous of families. You aren't necessarily to *blame* if your child has a drug problem, but once you know about it, you are *responsible* to help him or her overcome it.

So cry on your best friend's shoulder, chop wood, seek out a counselor, clean house, take deep breaths, or do whatever it takes to harness your emotions. Don't let your hurt and anger drive a further wedge between you and your child.

Once you've dealt with your own emotions, the next step is to determine the extent of the drug use. How you'll handle your child's situation will depend on how serious you think it to be. For the purposes of this discussion, I've divided drug use into three stages: experimental; regular or fairly frequent use that has not yet caused other serious problems; and heavy drug use that is affecting the youngster's health, personality, education, family relationships, or other areas of life.

DEALING WITH EXPERIMENTAL DRUG USE

You obviously won't send a child who's smoked a first joint off to a distant treatment center. Chances are you won't even know about it. If you find evidence of beginning drug use — perhaps some marijuana seeds or papers or a strange pill or capsule — you may need to do little more than bring it to the child's attention. Mention the specific evidence you have of drug use. Encourage (but don't nag) the child to tell you about it, including why and under what circumstances the drugs were used, and how he or she feels about it. (The youngster may be having mixed or bad feelings that need to be aired. On the other hand, insistent questioning can hamper communication by putting the child on the defensive. Don't make your kids feel as if they're on the witness stand.) Next, simply tell your child that drug use is a behavior you cannot permit in your family. Mention the health hazards and the danger to physical and emotional development during the adolescent years.

Make sure all your children understand that drug use is off limits for your family. Reaffirm your love and support and the confidence you have in your children. Reassure them also that you don't plan to bug them about the subject. On the other hand, tell them that you understand the pressures to use drugs are strong, and remind them you're available for help and counsel when they need you. Then drop the subject, continuing to keep your eyes and ears open, and to work on your all-around family relationships. If the drug use continues, use one of the methods described below.

REGULAR OR FREQUENT DRUG USE

You may or may not find definite physical evidence (marijuana, pills, drug paraphernalia, and so on) that your child is drifting into regular drug use. Many of the symptoms will be indirect and easy to confuse with the "normal" problems of adolescence. Still, you will want to watch closely if your child suddenly develops a pattern of falling grades, change in personality, listlessness (or hyperactivity), defensive or deceptive behavior, and/or the beginnings of withdrawal from the family. You may notice glazed eyes or smell marijuana (or deodorizer) on the youngster's breath. (For other symptoms, see chapter three.)

If you suspect, but don't have definite evidence of drug use, you may want to approach your child indirectly: "You seem troubled; what can I do to help you?" Remember drugs aren't the only problem young people are plagued by. It's a good idea to arrange for the child to see a doctor to make sure the problem isn't illness. On the other hand, if you're pretty sure drug use is involved, why not ask the kid about it? ("I've noticed *these specific symptoms* and I have to wonder if you're using drugs of some kind?")

If you're certain there is drug use, tell the youngster that you know about it. Again, give your child an opportunity to air feelings. Express your own feelings without using them as weapons. That is, you might say "I'm worried and confused about your drug use," but not "How do you always manage to make us sick with worry?" Also to be avoided is the "Why are you hurting us like this?" routine. Instead, try "We are upset that you may be hurting yourself." If there is disagreement about drug safety, arrange to get information from a source you can agree upon.

Restate or clarify the family rules on drug use. Reaffirm your love and support, along with your determination that the problem be resolved.

Now that the problem is on the table, your family has some options to choose from. There are several ways to deal with intermediate drug use. Those I will describe include professional counseling; a cooperative effort of a parent peer group; a program in which an individual parent or set of parents directly supervises the child's life for a while; and a method based on a family problem-solving technique.

When Is Professional Treatment Needed? There are at least four situations in which I think professional treatment should be considered:

1) when a school counselor, law enforcement official, or other authority recommends it. (If you don't agree with the official's assessment, get a second professional opinion.)

2) when drug use is causing other problems such as falling grades, truancy, withdrawal from family life, poor health, or other troubling changes.

3) when family relationships are strained or broken.

4) when you have doubt about your own ability to handle your child's drug use. (In this case, it may be most effective to get help for yourself.)

Over and over, drug counselors stress the importance of getting help *early*. Drug problems are much easier to treat before they're out of hand. Even if you choose one of the do-it-yourself methods for helping your child overcome drug use, you'll benefit from help and support for yourself. Many drug treatment and prevention agencies offer assistance to parents trying to cope with their children's drug use. (I'll discuss choosing a treatment center a little later.) Your clergyman, local parent group, or a family therapist also may be helpful.

Another resource available in some communities is Families Anonymous, a self-help group offering support to parents, spouses, and friends of people with drug-related problems. Weekly group meetings follow a program patterned after Alcoholics Anonymous and Al-Anon. While many parents attend because of their children's drug involvement, some come out of worry about truancy, delinquency, running away, or other behavior problems. Parents are welcome if they only suspect a problem.

Families Anonymous focuses on the feelings, attitudes, actions, and reactions of those affected by a family member's problem. Parents who've attended FA have found that getting their own acts together often makes it easier for their children to make positive changes. If you want to locate or start a group, write to the address listed at the end of this chapter for an information packet ($2).

The Parent Peer Group Method. The first parent networks were set up to counter drug use in adolescent friendship circles. In her book, *Parents Peers and Pot*, Marsha Manatt describes the experiences of one group of parents who successfully fought their young teenagers' drug use. Once they had the facts, the group set up common rules and restrictions among their children. Outings were supervised, curfews were observed, and places notorious for drug use were declared off limits. Telephone callers were asked to identify themselves to parents. Kids were given more home responsibilities. And no drugs, alcohol, or tobacco were permitted. At the same time, the parents made an all-out effort to reintroduce their kids to wholesome entertainment, activities, and service projects. In addition to overcoming drug use, parents give the program credit for breaking down the wall they found between the adolescent and adult worlds. For a complete description, see *Parents Peers and Pot*, available from the National Clearinghouse for Drug Abuse Information (address at the end of this chapter).

The Voth Approach. Dr. Harold Voth, a psychiatrist at the Menninger Foundation in Topeka, Kansas, advocates a rigorous approach to serious drug abuse in which parents temporarily take over complete responsibility for their children's lives. Children are driven to and picked up after school and never left at home alone. All afterschool activities, except those supervised by a parent or substitute, are suspended.

Dr. Voth wisely advises parents to treat their children with love and compassion during his program and to provide other gratifications in place of drugs. I would add that the method should be undertaken with great care, preferably with the help of a counselor or support group, in order not to damage family relationships. As soon as possible, I think the reins should be handed back over to the kids. I'd also concentrate on building children's skills (see chapter seven) to run their own lives successfully. Remember that once they're off to work or college, young people must be able to function without their parents. Dr. Voth describes his program in a booklet, *How To Get Your Child Off Marijuana*, available for $3 from the Citizens for Informed Choices on Marijuana (address at the end of the chapter).

Family Problem Solving. Parents who use this technique ask their kids to help design soluticns to family problems. The method is based on the premise that people are better motivated to carry out plans they've had a share in making. Dr. Thomas Gordon, who describes the strategy at length (although not specifically in terms of drug use) in his books, *P.E.T. — Parent Effectiveness Training* and *P.E.T. in Action* (Wyden Books, 1970 and 1976), calls it the "no-lose" method. Parents are taught to use the method in Parent Effectiveness Training courses. Family problem solving is also discussed by Adele Faber and Elaine Mazlish in their book, *How To Talk So Kids Will Listen and Listen So Kids Will Talk* (described in the bibliography).

The procedure should be introduced in a calm, positive atmosphere after family emotions have recovered from the shock of discovering drug use. Some skill in family communication, with an emphasis on listening, is a requirement. Allow plenty of time for the family planning session, which doesn't need to be as formal as the following description suggests. You can adapt the method to your family's own style of operation, although it is important to cover all the steps.

1) Parents and kids discuss the problem in terms of their respective needs and feelings at a family meeting. In the case of drug involvement, parents would probably say that they cannot permit drug use because of its various dangers (some of which they would spell out) and that they are worried about the well-being of their children.

2) Both kids and parents suggest ways that the problem might be dealt with. All proposals (no matter how impractical) are accepted for consideration and written down, without discussion. This rule is important: don't debate the merits of a suggestion until all are on the floor.

3) The family discusses the options they've listed to find one or more (or a compromise) they all can live with. As each suggestion is considered, all members are given an opportunity to explain why it is or is not acceptable to them. Nonthreatening language ("I'm not comfortable with that idea because ... ") is important at this point. No accusations or put-downs ("That won't work because you always ... ") are permitted.

One issue that should be on the agenda is how the young person will deal with his or her peer group. Some possibilities: enlisting the help of an old friend who does not use drugs, changing schools, joining a school organization whose members tend to be drug-free, talking with an adult or peer counselor, attending the school self-help group for people with alcohol or drug problems, or coming up with a reason ("I've decided to go out for the track team") that is acceptable to peers.

4) The family works out a step-by-step strategy for carrying out its plan, including who will do what and, in some cases, within which period of time.

5) The family gets together from time to time to evaluate its progress and, if necessary, to revise the plan. The

original conference should end on a note of confidence that the strategy will succeed. But if it doesn't, advocates of the plan suggest at least one more try before imposing a unilateral plan to deal with the drug use. I'd also recommend reading more about family problem solving in one of the books I've mentioned, as well as talking with a counselor or support group while you're guiding a family problem-solving project. If drug use continues, I'd get professional help for the child.

IF YOUR CHILD IS IN TROUBLE

If your child is already in serious trouble with drugs, many of this book's suggestions up to now may seem pretty elementary to you — like being told to practice good health habits when you've just been hit by a freight train. You may feel that your family relationships have broken down and that your communication could more accurately be called fights. Your home life may have disintegrated into a constant parent-child struggle that everyone is losing.

Serious drug problems almost always intensify other problems. They're like enormous potholes on the adolescent's road to independence, making the trip rough and treacherous for everyone, including parents. At such a point, the only reasonable course is to call in the professionals to help repair the road.

When there is a serious drug or alcohol situation in your family, it is important to recognize your limitations. You may not be able to deal with such a complex problem on your own. In fact, you may need to concentrate on the emotional problems the crisis is evoking in you — or between you and your spouse. Both you and your child may need professional help, as well as support from friends, relatives, clergymen, and others.

John Toto, director of The Bridge Therapeutic Center in Philadelphia, asks me to remind parents that a drug or alcohol problem requiring treatment is not the end of the world. "Here at The Bridge," he writes, "we have seen many parents and youth in treatment begin to do things for the first time that result in a good relationship." Unlikely as it may seem at the beginning, the whole family may eventually benefit from working through and learning from a difficult experience.

THE VARIETY OF DRUG AND ALCOHOL TREATMENT CENTERS.

The largest single trend I've noticed among treatment centers is an insistence that the family be involved in treatment. This practice stems from understanding that families can unknowingly contribute to drug problems, that drug problems in turn can damage the family, and that family health and support is essential to the recovery of the person in treatment.

Some residential treatment centers ask parents not to visit their children for the first few weeks, in order to let kids begin treatment free of the excess baggage of family tension. Very soon, however, the family becomes involved in the process. Family participation may take the form of family therapy (in which the family meets as a unit with a therapist), parent classes or therapy (in which parents work through some of their common problems together and support each other), or family/patient projects (in which families begin to function together once again). One family-oriented agency in my own community requires that parents devote a full week to sharing their child's treatment.

Beyond their common emphasis on the family, treatment centers are as varied as the people they're helping. Here are some of the differences I've noticed:

Structure. Agencies range from store-front centers where young people can walk in for a session or two without an appointment to campus-style residential centers, complete with their own schools, where treatment may last more than a year. In between, there are outpatient programs offering weekly to daily counseling; day-care programs where the young person may spend five days a week in treatment, going home evenings and weekends; and community or hospital residential programs, where the drug-dependent person may be admitted for several weeks of intensive treatment. Many treatment agencies also have hot lines (check your yellow pages) or other crisis services, and almost all hospitals offer emergency treatment.

Cost. The cost of treatment ranges from absolutely free to very expensive. Agencies that accept public funding almost always have "sliding-scale" fees — that is, their charges are based on your ability to pay. Many drug and alcohol treatment programs qualify for coverage by health and hospital insurance. The total cost of treatment is almost always lower if the problem is caught at an early stage.

Professional Staff. Staff members may include doctors, psychologists, social workers, teachers, therapists, nurses, clergymen, volunteer workers and/or many others. Some organizations train people who have recovered from alcohol or drug problems to help in the treatment of others.

Goals. Some agencies aim for a totally drug-free person at the end of treatment. Others are satisfied to reduce the person's drug use to the point that he or she can function fairly normally in the home, at school or work, and in the community.

Understanding of Drug Use. Agencies may approach drug/alcohol dependence as a disease, as a psychological malfunction, or as a "holistic" problem (that is, having multiple causes that involve the whole physical, psychological, social, and spiritual person). In actual practice, there is a good deal of overlap among these positions.

Treatment Methods. Complete treatment programs include at least four stages: 1) diagnosis and evaluation of the problem; 2) detoxification (medical treatment for physical dependence), if needed; 3) the actual treatment process; and 4) an arrangement for aftercare or a post-treatment support group. The treatment phase of most programs includes some form of individual, group, or family counseling. Beyond that, methods vary. Some agencies offer several approaches, which they tailor to or even plan with the help of the troubled person.

Many hospitals and other agencies are using the time-tested program developed by Alcoholics Anonymous. Others feature recreational, camping, or work projects specially structured to provide practice in problem solving, interpersonal relationships, decision making, stress management and other skills that promote independent living. There may be classes on drug effects, nutrition, body processes, and related topics. Some agencies offer vocational training. Many feature recreational activities to help young people enjoy life without dependence on chemicals. A large number of treatment centers help their enrollees learn to organize their leisure time, which may have been devoted almost entirely to drugs in the past. Church-related agencies often stress religious training.

Campus-style programs create little communities in which young people work, play, go to school, and live together. These communities are often structured to mirror or even exaggerate conditions in the real world. They emphasize helping the troubled person find and experience nonchemical support. Residents may be given opportunities to earn recognition; experience friendship and positive peer pressure; enjoy family-style support, affection, and cooperation; learn to accept responsibility for their own behavior; assume leadership; arrive at educational and vocational goals; and practice other skills for independent, drug-free living.

How to Locate and Choose a Treatment Center. A *National Directory of Drug Abuse and Alcoholism Treatment Programs* is available (one copy free) from the National Clearinghouse for Drug Abuse Information. As a source of local programs, however, I've found the yellow pages of the phone book more up-to-date and complete. Some states and school districts also have compiled their own directories. Members of parent groups, school officials, and clergymen often have information (or at least opinions) about which programs have been most effective.

When you're shopping for treatment centers, read their literature and talk with their representatives. Drug counselors themselves caution never to place a child in an agency you haven't visited. It's important that you feel comfortable with and confident in the treatment counselor. Since treatment won't work without your child's cooperation, his or her reaction to the counselor is even more important (although many kids resist *anyone* at the beginning).

I wouldn't be too concerned about the exact nature of the counselor's educational background. Although proper training obviously is important, sensitivity and experience mean a great deal. Some excellent counselors have undergraduate or even technical school training.

I would be extremely wary of anyone who promised a fast or definite "cure." Drug treatment is a difficult, uncertain business, in which a great deal depends on the motivation of the patient. No one can guarantee an outcome.

You might use the preceding section on the differences in treatment centers to compile a list of features you think important for your own child. Here are some things I would look for:

● *A positive, supportive climate.* Although I understand that learning and change are often painful, I would want the basic philosophy of the treatment center to emphasize respect, affection, and support for the person in treatment.

● *Drug-free objectives.* If my child had cancer, I might eventually be happy to settle for *remission* (since no one has a perfect success rate), but I would want a doctor who intended to attempt a *cure.* I would apply the same reasoning to a drug treatment agency.

● *Attention to life skills.* I would want my child's treatment to include opportunities to catch up on communication, decision making, problem solving, and related skills that he or she probably missed out on earlier because of drug involvement.

• *Family involvement in treatment, or at least a parent support group.* I would want to get my own life and emotions in order and be able to contribute to a more constructive family life for everyone (including me) after the treatment period.

• *Arrangements for aftercare.* I would expect my child to return to the treatment center for regular sessions or to be enrolled in a community support group after treatment. If he or she has been away from home in a residential center, I would be concerned about its "reentry plan." The final phase of treatment should concentrate on transition to life in the outside world which, unlike the treatment center, does not revolve around the support and protection of my child. Understanding that my family would need to readjust to each other, I would want a support group for myself and my spouse during the adjustment period.

A caution: the first treatment your family chooses may not succeed. Different families need different treatment methods. But the stakes are high enough to keep trying: if one treatment doesn't work, look for another. Before you do, though, have a talk with your child to try to figure out what was lacking in the first attempt. It may have been inadequate aftercare ("I couldn't hack it on my own when I got back to the old school") or lack of family treatment ("I still can't talk to you without getting a lecture"). It may be that your youngster has become skillful at conning counselors and needs an especially shrewd one. He or she may need more help with problem solving, decision making or other skills for living. Once you've analyzed the situation, choose a new treatment agency geared to supply whatever you've decided was missing in the first experience.

One residential center I'm aware of (there may be others) that functions as a "last resort" is Elan, at Poland Spring, Maine. Most of the residents of Elan have gone from treatment to treatment, unsuccessfully. Their parents have usually been desperate to find help for their children, who have been chronically in trouble. Elan describes its program as tough and demanding, but supportive. If you're at your wits' end about your child's persistent drug involvement, you may want to consider a center like Elan.

ON THE BRIGHTER SIDE

Distressful as it is, the drug problem may be having one positive side effect. It is encouraging a lot of us to take a fresh look at the way we're raising our children. As we do, we're learning that preparing kids for the obstacle course of the 1980s requires special effort on the part of parents. Rearing children can't be undertaken as matter-of-factly as it once was.

We're also learning, sometimes much to our surprise, that parents are far from powerless. We can call upon a number of effective resources, both within and outside the home, to discourage drug use. Some of us are even discovering that drug problems in our own homes aren't necessarily the ultimate disaster. Many families have resolved them and have found themselves not only intact but stronger and more united for having shared the challenge.

We may not be able to overcome the national drug problem in time to help the current generation of children. But there is a great deal that we can do. We can educate ourselves, so that drugs are no longer shrouded in mystery for us. We can support the efforts of government and other public agencies to control the supply of drugs. We can lobby for sound legislation as well as funds for prevention, treatment, and law enforcement agencies.

We can confront problems that arise in our families, getting help when we need it. We can support each other and create new communities to undergird ourselves and our children. Above all, we can give our kids unqualified love and acceptance, along with opportunities to develop their own capacities to handle not only drugs, but all the problems — old, new, and yet to be imagined — they will face in life.

DISCUSSION GUIDE

The following questions can be used to stimulate thought or discussion among people who are using the book as a group resource.

Chapter One

1. What do you think your first reaction would be if you discovered your child using drugs? Alcohol? Did your answers reveal any differences in the way you feel about these similarly dangerous substances?

2. What do you regard as the most frightening result of adolescent drug use?

3. What other problems among adolescents are you personally aware of that suggest all is not well in the age-group?

4. Dr. Stephen Glenn and others believe that the high rates of adolescent drug abuse, suicide, violence, unwanted pregnancy and other difficulties are all parts of a larger problem. If you agree, what factors do you believe to be at the root of the larger problem? If you disagree, how do you think the various individual problems are related?

5. What do you think is the most important way parents can discourage drug use in their children?

Chapter Two

1. How many commercials for pain remedies were you able to count during one evening of prime-time TV programming?

2. Can you think of a "drugs are okay" message (consider prescription and over-the-counter products) you may have sent your children recently?

3. Suppose that you were to keep a record of the meaningful time that you spend in common activities or conversation with your children during the next week. What do you think your record would reveal?

4. Think about the responsibilities your children regularly fulfill in your family. Would you rate most of these as essential, fairly important, or nonessential duties?

5. Can you think of a situation in which you could help or allow your child to bring about a change he or she considers important?

6. Describe an important family decision to which your children have made important contributions.

Chapter Three

1. How do you think the amount of drug use in your school or community compares with national averages? Are statistics available to check your impressions?

2. What changes do your children report noticing in people who are headed for trouble with drugs?

3. How would you rate your influence over your children in comparison to the influence of their peers? Does this represent a change since you were an adolescent?

4. What factors do you think accounted for the influence your parents may have exerted over you as an adolescent? Would you regard these factors as positive or negative? Do you think there are better ways to achieve influence? If so, how?

5. A drug counselor wrote, "Teenage drug abuse is difficult to treat because kids *enjoy* the drugs." How can parents counter the enjoyment factor?

Chapter Four

1. How much alcohol consumption were you aware of among students when you were in high school? How much are you aware of today?

2. What can parents do to control opportunities (parties, etc.) for binge drinking?

3. Would you be willing to role play a parent explaining his or her reasons for abstinence from alcohol? For moderate drinking?

4. What ground rules do you think are necessary in a family whose children are permitted to drink moderately?

5. Can you think of an important decision your child made on his or her own recently that might help develop the decision-making skills he or she would need to decide against tobacco or other drugs?

Chapter Five

1. How would you open a conversation with a child you just caught smoking marijuana? What would you hope to accomplish in such a conversation? What would you want to avoid?

2. Part of the appeal of marijuana to young people may be its element of ritual. What other rituals are available to young people?

3. What can you do to insure that your children have accurate information about marijuana and other illicit drugs?

4. Many drug counselors believe the most serious effect of chronic marijuana use may be its interruption of personal and psychological development. Which dangers concern you the most?

5. What are your children able to report about cases of "marijuana burnout" among their classmates?

Chapter Six

1. Ask your children to list the drugs they know are being used in their schools. Compare your children's lists with those of others in the group. How many did the group come up with? Can you classify the drugs by drug families? Were some drugs mentioned that are not discussed in this book?

2. PCP and marijuana use began to decrease as their dangers were publicized. What does this suggest about the interest of young people in safety? About the importance of up-to-date drug data? How can you, your children, and your schools stay up-to-date?

3. How many substances can you find in your medicine cabinet, garage, basement, cupboards, and so on, that could be used as recreational drugs by young people?

4. Which drugs have you heard joked about or mentioned matter-of-factly on television or in the movies?

5. Which drugs are involved in most emergency problems and hospitalizations in your locality? (You can find out from a local hot line, drug information agency, or emergency treatment center.)

Chapter Seven

1. Can you list three specific things you could do as a parent to encourage each of the skills described as "needs of children" early in chapter seven?

2. How effective is the "network" among the parents of your children's friends? What could you do to improve it?

3. What kind of prevention or intervention programs are being conducted in or by your schools? What kind of help do they need?

4. Describe ways parents can discourage drug use in families, schools, or communities. Share and compare ideas within your group.

5. Which of the anti-drug programs described in chapter seven would be best suited to your group or community?

Chapter Eight

1. How sure are you that your children clearly understand your position on drug use? If you have doubts, how can you inform them without putting them on the defensive?

2. A school counselor has just told you that your child (whom you believe to be drug-free) needs help with a drug problem. How do you think you would react? What would you do first? Next?

3. What drug treatment agencies are available in your community? What do you know about them?

4. The family problem-solving technique is most likely to help with drug problems in families who have previous experience in the method. Can you identify another problem that your family might try to solve with the help of this approach?

5. The author's criteria for a drug treatment center are described in the chapter. What qualities would you insist upon in a treatment center?

WHERE TO WRITE FOR HELP OR INFORMATION

Alcoholics Anonymous
P.O. Box 459
Grand Central Station
New York, New York 10017

Al-Anon Family Groups
P.O. Box 182
Madison Square Station
New York, New York 10159

National Clearinghouse for
Alcohol Information
P.O. Box 2345
Rockville, Maryland 20852

The Alcohol Education Project
National Congress of Parents
and Teachers
700 North Rush Street
Chicago, Illinois 60611

National Clearinghouse for Drug
Abuse Information
P.O. Box 416
Kensington, Maryland 20795

National Federation of Parents
for Drug-Free Youth
P.O. Box 722
Silver Spring, Maryland 20901

Families Anonymous
P.O. Box 344
Torrance, California 90501

Parent Prevention Program
Project Pegasus Inc.
703 Welch Road, Suite H-4
Palo Alto, California 94304

or

Center for Human Development
3702 Mt. Diablo Boulevard
Lafayette, California 94549

Parents in Crisis Inc.
2205 Genesee Street
Buffalo, New York 14211

Citizens for Informed Choices
on Marijuana Inc.
P.O. Box 1245
Darien, Connecticut 06820

Elan One Corporation
RFD Box 33
Poland Springs, Maine 04274

The following organizations
offer parent-training courses:

American Guidance Service Inc.
(Systematic Training for
Effective Parenting)
Circle Pines, Minnesota 55014

Effectiveness Training Inc.
(Parent Effectiveness Training)
531 Stevens Avenue
Solana Beach, California 92075

Humansphere Inc.
(Developing Capable People)
P.O. Box 368
Station A
Mississauga, Ontario L5A 381

Addresses of local alcohol and drug treatment/prevention agencies, hot lines, and information centers are listed in phone directories under various headings beginning with "Alcohol" and "Drug."

SOME HELPFUL BOOKS

Berman, Eleanor. **The Cooperating Family.** Englewood Cliffs, New Jersey: Prentice-Hall, 1977.

A single working mother describes how her family organized itself to run their household. The author discovered that "allowing children to function at full capacity" not only got the work done, but helped them develop confidence, self-esteem, competence, and responsibility.

Delaine, John K. **Who's Raising the Family? A Workbook for Parents and Children.** Available at $5 (including postage and handling) from the Wisconsin Clearinghouse, 1954 East Washington Avenue, Madison, Wisconsin, 53704.

A workbook approach for "any parents who have ever worried about their children someday getting involved in drugs." Information and exercises help parents help children develop positive self-concepts, express feelings, make decisions and solve problems, and accept responsibility for their actions. The manual also presents some helpful parenting techniques.

Faber, Adele, and Mazlich, Elaine. **How To Talk So Kids Will Listen and Listen So Kids Will Talk.** New York: Rawson, Wade Publishers, Inc., 1980.

This book gives detailed practical instructions for improving communication with children. In addition to the outcome promised by the title, the authors offer help in coping with anger and other feelings, dealing with misbehavior, getting kids' cooperation, giving helpful praise, encouraging independence, and achieving a number of other goals of parenting.

Glenn, H. Stephen. **Strengthening the Family.** Bethesda, Maryland: Potomac Press, 1981. Available at $2.50 from the publisher, 7101 Wisconsin Avenue, Suite 1006, Bethesda, Maryland, 20014.

Dr. Glenn discusses the common ground of delinquency, teenage pregnancy, drug and alcohol dependence, and other problems that are plaguing adolescents. He recommends specific strategies parents can follow to reduce the risk of these problems to young people.

Kuzma, Kay, Ed.D. **Prime-Time Parenting.** New York: Rawson, Wade Publishers, Inc., 1980.

A working mother tells how to create quality time with children during the busiest years of a parent's life. Mrs. Kuzma combines sound philosophy with many practical suggestions, examples, exercises, and anecdotes. Although special attention is given to the concerns of working parents, the book is an excellent resource for anyone who's raising children.

Manatt, Marsha, PhD. **Parents Peers and Pot.** Rockville, Maryland: National Institute on Drug Abuse. Available, one copy free, from National Clearinghouse for Drug Abuse Information.

This book tells the story of one of the first "parent peer groups," organized to overcome drug use among young teenagers in a suburban Atlanta neighborhood. Dr. Manatt also discusses the evolution of the drug culture, the risks of marijuana, and a number of remedies based on "parent power."

Manning, William O. and Vinton, Jean. **Harmfully Involved.** Available at $4.95 from Hazelden Literature, Box 176, Center City, Minnesota, 55012.

An account of the development of one of the earliest school intervention efforts. Dr. Manning's program for intercepting drug and alcohol problems at the Wayzata, Minnesota, high school has been the model for many others around the country.

Myrick, Robert D. and Erney, Tom. **Caring and Sharing: Becoming a Peer Facilitator** and **Youth Helping Youth: A Handbook for Training Peer Facilitators.** Available at $6.95 each, softbound, from Educational Media Corporation, P.O. Box 21311, Minneapolis, Minnesota, 55421.

This set of books provides complete classroom materials and guidance for the leader of a peer helping program. It emphasizes preparing students to act as tutors, big brothers and sisters, or group discussion leaders. Although training is not specifically directed to drug prevention, it could easily be adapted. A set of books for training elementary students is also available.

Rusche, Sue. **How To Form a Families In Action Group in Your Community.** Available at $10 from Families in Action Inc., 3845 North Druid Hills Road, Suite 300, Decatur, Georgia, 30033.

This manual provides step-by-step instructions for organizing an activist parent group. Included are check lists, organizational charts, sample duties for twelve committees, articles of incorporation, and even an outline for a speech. The handbook also contains an account of the FAI experience and a number of anti-drug articles and speeches.